BENCHMARK SERIES

Microsoft®

office

2007

Office

Nita Rutkosky
Pierce College at Puyallup
Puyallup, Washington

Audrey Rutkosky Roggenkamp
Pierce College at Puyallup
Puyallup, Washington

Managing Editor	Sonja Brown
Senior Developmental Editor	Christine Hurney
Production Editor	Donna Mears
Cover and Text Designer	Leslie Anderson
Copy Editor	Susan Capecchi
Desktop Production	John Valo, Desktop Solutions
Proofreader	Laura Nelson
Indexer	Nancy Fulton

Acknowledgments: The authors and editors wish to thank the following individuals for checking the accuracy of the instruction and exercises:
- Catherine Caldwell, Technical Writer, Memphis, Tennessee
- Theresa Jabs, Computer Applications Tester, Farmington, Minnesota
- Robertt Neilly, Professor, Computer Applications, Humber College, Toronto, Canada
- Pamela J. Silvers, Chairperson, Business Computer Technologies, Asheville-Buncombe Technical Community College, Asheville, North Carolina

Care has been taken to verify the accuracy of information presented in this book. However, the authors, editors, and publisher cannot accept responsibility for Web, e-mail, newsgroup, or chat room subject matter or content, or for consequences from application of the information in this book, and make no warranty, expressed or implied, with respect to its content.

Photo Credits: Introduction page 1 (clockwise from top), Lexmark International, Inc., courtesy of Dell Inc., all rights Hewlett-Packard Company, Logitech, Micron Technology, Inc.; Word Level 1 page 3, Asia Images Group/AsiaPix/Getty Images, page 4, © Corbis: Excel Level 1 pages 1, 3, 4, © Corbis: Access Level 1 page 1, © Corbis; PowerPoint pages 1, 2, and 4, © Corbis; photos in Student Resources CD, courtesy of Kelly Rutkosky and Michael Rutkosky.

Trademarks: Microsoft is a trademark or registered trademark of Microsoft Corporation in the United States and/or other countries. Some of the product names and company names included in this book have been used for identification purposes only and may be trademarks or registered trade names of their respective manufacturers and sellers. The authors, editors, and publisher disclaim any affiliation, association, or connection with, or sponsorship or endorsement by, such owners.

We have made every effort to trace the ownership of all copyrighted material and to secure permission from copyright holders. In the event of any question arising as to the use of any material, we will be pleased to make the necessary corrections in future printings. Thanks are due to the aforementioned authors, publishers, and agents for permission to use the materials indicated.

ISBN 978-0-76382-983-4 (Text)
ISBN 978-0-76382-999-5 (Text + CD)

© 2008 by Paradigm Publishing, Inc.
875 Montreal Way
St. Paul, MN 55102
E-mail: educate@emcp.com
Web site: www.emcp.com

Printed in the United States of America

16 15 14 13 12 11 10 09 08 07   1 2 3 4 5 6 7 8 9 10

CONTENTS

These activities appear at the end of every chapter.

office
Contents

iii

office

office
Contents

Benchmark Microsoft Office 2007 is designed for students who want to learn how to use the new version of Microsoft's popular suite to enhance their productivity for educational, workplace, and home use. Throughout this text, students are expected to develop and execute strategies for solving information processing and management problems using Word 2007; for solving numeric and mathematical problems using Excel 2007; for organizing, querying, and retrieving data using Access 2007; and for writing, creating, and producing presentations using PowerPoint 2007. After successfully completing a course using this textbook, students will be able to

- Analyze, synthesize, and evaluate school, work, or home information-processing tasks and use application software to meet those needs efficiently and effectively
- Access the Internet and use the browse, search, and hyperlink capabilities of Web browsers
- Create, design, and produce professional documents using word processing software
- Process, manipulate, and represent numeric data using spreadsheet software
- Plan, structure, and create databases for efficient data access and retrieval using database software
- Use presentation software to design and create informational and motivational slide shows that contain hyperlinks, tables, images, and animation
- Learn strategies for merging and integrating source data from different applications

In addition to mastering essential Word, Excel, Access, and PowerPoint skills, students will learn the basic features and functions of computer hardware, the Windows Vista operating system, and Internet Explorer 7.0. Upon completing the text, they can expect to be proficient in using the major applications of the Office 2007 suite to organize, analyze, and present information.

Achieving Proficiency in Office 2007

Since its inception several Office versions ago, the Benchmark Series has served as a standard of excellence in software instruction. Elements of the book function individually and collectively to create an inviting, comprehensive learning environment that produces successful computer users. On this and following pages, take a visual tour of the structure and features that comprise the highly popular Benchmark model.

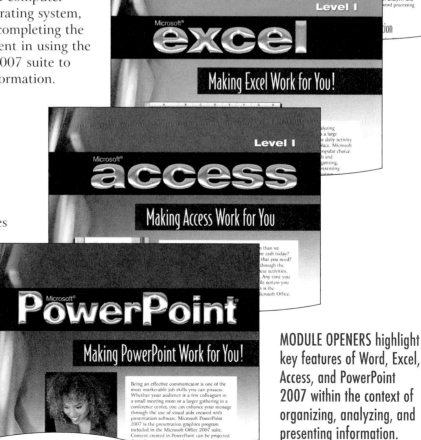

MODULE OPENERS highlight key features of Word, Excel, Access, and PowerPoint 2007 within the context of organizing, analyzing, and presenting information.

UNIT OPENERS display the unit's four chapter titles. Each program module has two units, which conclude with a comprehensive unit performance assessment.

CHAPTER OPENERS present the Performance Objectives and highlight the practical relevance of the skills students will learn.

CD icon identifies a folder of data files to be copied to student's storage medium.

SNAP icon alerts students to corresponding SNAP tutorial titles.

New! PROJECT APPROACH organizes instruction and practice into multipart projects that focus on related program features.

Project overview identifies tasks to accomplish and the key features to use in completing the work.

PROJECT APPROACH: Builds Skill Mastery within Realistic Context

Each project exercise guides students step by step to the desired outcome. Screen captures illustrate what the screen should look like at key points.

Typically, a file remains open throughout a project. Students save their work incrementally.

Between project parts, the text presents instruction on the features and skills necessary to accomplish the next task.

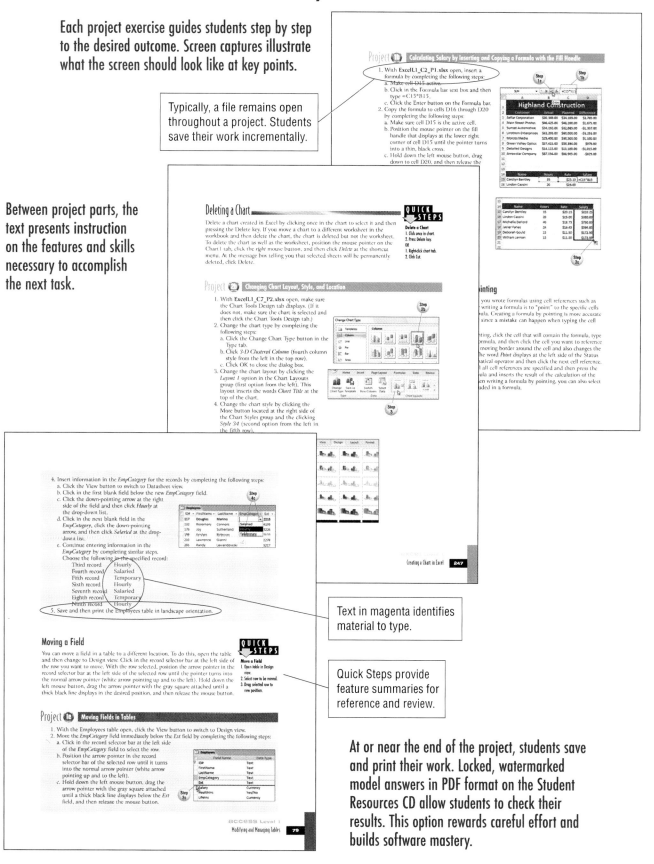

Text in magenta identifies material to type.

Quick Steps provide feature summaries for reference and review.

At or near the end of the project, students save and print their work. Locked, watermarked model answers in PDF format on the Student Resources CD allow students to check their results. This option rewards careful effort and builds software mastery.

CHAPTER REVIEW ACTIVITIES: A Hierarchy of Learning Assessments

CHAPTER summary

- Use the spelling feature to check spelling of slides in a presentation. Begin the spelling checker by clicking the Review tab and then clicking the Spelling button in the Proofing group.
- Refer to Table 2.1 for methods for selecting text in slides.
- Text in a placeholder is positioned inside of a placeholder. Click in a placeholder to select the placeholder and position the insertion point inside.
- Display the Find dialog box by clicking the Find button in the Editing group in the Home tab.
- Display the Replace dialog box by clicking the Replace button in the Editing group in the Home tab.
- With buttons in the Clipboard group or with optio[...] you can cut and paste or copy and paste text in sli[...]
- You can use the mouse to move text in the Slides/O[...] and then drag it to a new location or hold down th[...] copy text to a new location.
- Use the sizing handles that display around a select[...] decrease the size of the placeholder. You can use th[...] placeholder to a new location in the slide.
- Use the New Slide button in the Home tab to inse[...]
- Delete a selected slide by clicking the Delete butto[...] Home tab or by pressing the Delete button.
- You can move or delete a selected slide in Normal [...] pane or in Slide Sorter view.
- Copy a selected slide by holding down the Ctrl key[...] the desired location.
- Use the Copy and Paste buttons in the Clipboard g[...] copy a slide between presentations.
- Select adjacent slides in the Slides/Outline pane or[...] clicking the first slide, holding down the Shift key, [...] slide. Select nonadjacent slides by holding down th[...] each desired slide.
- Duplicate slides in a presentation by selecting th[...] Slides/Outline pane, clicking the New Slide button [...] the *Duplicate Selected Slides* option.
- You can copy slides from a presentation into the op[...] at the Reuse Slides task pane. Display this task pa[...] button arrow and then clicking *Reuse Slides* at the [...]
- Display a presentation in Print Preview by clicking [...] to *Print*, and then clicking *Print Preview*.

CHAPTER SUMMARY captures the purpose and execution of key features.

- In Print Preview, display the Header and Footer dialog box by clicking the Options button and then clicking *Header and Footer* at the drop-down list. Use options in the dialog box to insert the date and time, a header, a footer, slide numbers, or page numbers. The options will vary depending on which tab is selected—*Slide* or *Notes and Handouts*.
- Click the Help button in a dialog box and the PowerPoint Help window displays with information specific to the dialog box.
- Click the Microsoft Office Word Help button or press F1 to display the PowerPoint Help window.

COMMANDS review

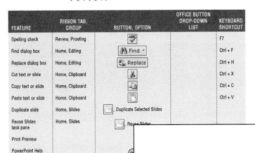

FEATURE	RIBBON TAB, GROUP	BUTTON, OPTION	OFFICE BUTTON DROP-DOWN LIST	KEYBOARD SHORTCUT
Spelling check	Review, Proofing			F7
Find dialog box	Home, Editing	Find		Ctrl + F
Replace dialog box	Home, Editing	Replace		Ctrl + H
Cut text or slide	Home, Clipboard			Ctrl + X
Copy text or slide	Home, Clipboard			Ctrl + C
Paste text or slide	Home, Clipboard			Ctrl + V
Duplicate slide	Home, Slides	Duplicate Selected Slides		
Reuse Slides task pane	Home, Slides	Reuse Slides		
Print Preview				
PowerPoint Help window				

COMMANDS REVIEW summarizes visually the major features and alternative methods of access.

CONCEPTS check

Test Your Knowledge

Completion: In the space provided at the right, indicate the correct term, symbol, or command.

1. The Spelling button is located in the Proofing group in this tab.

2. This is the keyboard shortcut to select all text in a placeholder.

3. The Find button is located in this group in the Home tab.

4. In the Slides/Outline pane with the Outline tab selected, hold down the left mouse button on this to select all text in the slide.

5. To copy text to a new location in the Slides/Outline pane with the Outline tab selected, hold down this key while dragging text.

6. The border of a selected placeholder displays these handles as well as a green rotation handle.

7. You can reorganize slides in a presentation in the Slides/Outline pane or in this view.

8. You can copy selected slides in a presentation using this option from the New Slide button drop-down list.

9. To select adjacent slides, click the first slide, hold down this key, and then click the last slide.

10. Click the New Slide button arrow and then click the *Reuse Slides* option at the drop-down list and this displays.

11. Display the presentation in Print Preview by clicking the Office button, pointing to this option, and then clicking *Print Preview*.

12. In Print Preview, display the Header and Footer dialog box by clicking this button in the Print Preview tab and then clicking *Header and Footer* at the drop-down list.

13. This is the keyboard shortcut to display the PowerPoint Help window.

CONCEPTS CHECK questions assess knowledge recall.

SKILLS check

Demonstrate Your Proficiency

Assessment

1 CREATE AN ELECTRONIC DESIGN PRESENTATION

1. Create the presentation shown in Figure 2.7 using a design theme of your choosing. (When typing bulleted text, press the Tab key to move the insertion point to the desired tab level.)
2. After creating the slides, complete a spelling check on the text in the slides.
3. Save the presentation into the PowerPoint2007C2 folder on your storage medium and name the presentation **PP_C2_A1**.
4. Run the presentation.
5. Preview the presentation, change the *Print What* option to *Handouts (4 Slides Per Page)*, change the orientation to landscape, and then print the presentation.
6. Make the following changes to the presentation:
   a. Change to Slide Sorter view and then move Slide 3 between Slides 1 and 2.
   b. Move Slide 4 between Slides 2 and 3.
   c. Search for the word *document* and replace it with the word *brochure*. (Make Slide 1 active and then capitalize the "b" in "brochure.")
   d. Add a transition and sound of your choosing to each slide.
7. Save the presentation.
8. Display the Reuse Slides task pane, browse to the PowerPoint2007C2 folder on your storage medium, and then double-click **LayoutTips.pptx**.
9. Insert the *Layout Punctuation Tips* slide below Slide 4.
10. Insert the *Layout Tips* slide below Slide 5.
11. Close the Reuse Slides task pane.
12. Find all occurrences of *Layout* and replace with *Design*. (Insert a check mark in the *Match case* check box.)
13. Move Slide 5 between Slides 1 and 2.
14. Move Slide 6 between Slides 2 and 3.
15. Save the presentation.
16. Print the presentation as a handout with six slides per page.
17. Close **PP_C2_A1.pptx**.

SKILLS CHECK exercises ask students to develop both standard and customized kinds of word processing, spreadsheet, database, or presentation documents without how-to directions.

Chapter Two

CASE study

Apply Your Skills

Part 1

You are the office manager at the Company Connections agency. One of your responsibilities is to conduct workshops for preparing individuals for the job search process. A coworker has given you a presentation for the workshop but the presentation needs some editing and modifying. Open **JobAnalysis.pptx** and then save the presentation and name it **PP_C2_CS_P1**. Check each slide in the presentation and then make modifications to maintain consistency in the size and location of placeholders (consider using the Reset button to reset the formatting and size of the placeholders), maintain consistency in heading text, move text from an overcrowded slide to a new slide, complete a spelling check, apply a design theme, and make any other modifications to improve the presentation. Save **PP_C2_CS_P1.pptx**.

Part 2

After reviewing the presentation, you realize that you need to include slides on resumes. Open the **ResumePresentation.pptx** presentation and then copy Slides 2 and 3 into the PP_C2_CS_P1.pptx presentation. You want to add additional information on resume writing tips and decide to use the Internet to find information. Locate information on the Internet with tips on writing a resume and then create a slide (or two) with the information you find. Add a transition and sound to all slides in the presentation. Save the **PP_C2_CS_P1.pptx** presentation.

Part 3

You know that Microsoft Word offers a number of resume templates you can download from the Microsoft Office Online site. You decide to include information in the presentation on how to download resumes. Open Microsoft Word, click the Office button, and then click *New* at the drop-down list. At the New Document dialog box, click the Help button that displays in the upper right corner of the dialog box. Read the information on downloading templates and then experiment with downloading a template. With the PP_C2_CS_P1.pptx presentation open, add an additional slide to the end of the presentation that provides steps on how to download a resume in Microsoft Word. Print the presentation as a handout with six slides per page. Save, run, and then close the **PP_C2_CS_P1.pptx** presentation.

The chapter CASE STUDY requires analyzing a workplace scenario and then planning and executing multipart projects to meet the information needs.

Students search the Web and/or use the Help feature to locate additional information required to complete the Case Study.

powerpoint
Modifying a Presentation and Using Help   **73**

office
Preface   **xiii**

UNIT PERFORMANCE ASSESSMENT: Cross-Disciplinary, Comprehensive Evaluation

ASSESSING PROFICIENCY
checks mastery of features.

WRITING ACTIVITIES involve
applying program skills in
a communication context.

INTERNET RESEARCH
project reinforces
research and
information
processing skills.

JOB STUDY at the end of Unit 2
presents a capstone assessment
requiring critical thinking and
problem solving.

An **INTEGRATED PROJECT** at the end of
the text offers students the opportunity to
experience the power of using the Office
suite—importing and exporting data among
the major applications to meet information
processing needs most effectively.

Student Courseware

Student Resources CD Each Benchmark Series textbook is packaged with a Student Resources CD containing the data files required for completing the projects and assessments. A CD icon and folder name displayed on the opening page of chapters reminds students to copy a folder of files from the CD to the desired storage medium before beginning the project exercises. Directions for copying folders are printed on the inside back cover. The Student Resources CD also contains the model answers in PDF format for the project exercises within chapters. Files are locked and watermarked, but students can compare their completed documents with the PDF files, either on screen or in hard copy (printed) format.

Internet Resource Center Additional learning tools and reference materials are available at the book-specific Web site at www.emcp.net/BenchmarkOffice07Vista. Students can locate and use the same resources that are on the Student Resources CD along with study aids, Web links, and tips for working with computers effectively in academic and workplace settings.

SNAP Training and Assessment SNAP is a Web-based program that provides hands-on instruction, practice, and testing for learning Microsoft Office 2007 and Windows. SNAP course work simulates operations of Office 2007. The program is comprised of a Web-based learning management system, multimedia tutorials, performance skill items, a concept test bank, and online grade book and course planning tools. A CD-based set of tutorials teaching the basics of Office and Windows is also available for additional practice not requiring Internet access.

Class Connections Available for both WebCT and Blackboard e-learning platforms, Paradigm's Class Connection provides self-quizzes and study aids and facilitates communication among students and instructors via e-mail and e-discussion.

Instructor Resources

Curriculum Planner and Resources Instructor support for the Benchmark Series has been expanded to include a *Curriculum Planner and Resources* binder with CD. This all-in-one print resource includes planning resources such as Lesson Blueprints, teaching hints, and sample course syllabi; presentation resources such as PowerPoint presentations and handouts; and assessment resources including an overview of assessment venues, live program and PDF model answers for intrachapter projects, and live program and annotated PDF model answers for end-of-chapter and end-of-unit assessments. Contents of the *Curriculum Planner and Resources* binder are also available on the Instructor's CD and on the password-protected Instructor's section of the Internet Resource Center for this title at www.emcp.com.

Computerized Test Generator Instructors can use ExamView test generating software and the provided bank of multiple-choice items to create customized Web-based or print tests.

System Requirements

This text is designed for the student to complete projects and assessments on a computer running a standard installation of Microsoft Office 2007, Professional Edition, and the Microsoft Windows Vista (Home Premium, Business, or Ultimate) operating system. To effectively run this suite and operating system, your computer should be outfitted with the following:

- 1 gigahertz (GHz) processor or higher; 1 gigabyte (GB) of RAM
- DVD drive
- 15 GB of available hard-disk space
- 1024 by 768 monitor resolution *Note: Screen captures in this book were created using 1024 by 768 resolution; screens with higher resolution may look different.*
- Computer mouse or compatible pointing device

About the Authors

Nita Rutkosky began teaching business education courses at Pierce College in Puyallup, Washington, in 1978. Since then she has taught a variety of software applications to students in postsecondary Information Technology certificate and degree programs. In addition to co-authoring texts in the *Benchmark Office 2007 Series*, she has co-authored *Signature Word 2007*, *Marquee Office 2007*, and *Using Computers in the Medical Office: Microsoft Word, Excel, and PowerPoint 2003*. Other textbooks she has written for Paradigm Publishing include books on previous versions of Microsoft Office along with WordPerfect, desktop publishing, keyboarding, and voice recognition.

Audrey Rutkosky Roggenkamp has been teaching courses in the Business Information Technology department at Pierce College in Puyallup including keyboarding, skill building, and Microsoft Office programs. In addition to titles in the *Benchmark Office 2007 Series*, she has co-authored *Using Computers in the Medical Office*, *Marquee Office 2007*, and *Signature Word 2007*.

Getting Started in Office 2007

In this textbook, you will learn to operate several computer application programs that combine to make an application "suite." This suite of programs is called Microsoft Office 2007. The programs you will learn to operate are the software, which includes instructions telling the computer what to do. Some of the application programs in the suite include a word processing program named Word, a spreadsheet program named Excel, a database program named Access, and a presentation program named PowerPoint.

Identifying Computer Hardware

The computer equipment you will use to operate the suite of programs is referred to as hardware. You will need access to a microcomputer system that should consist of the CPU, monitor, keyboard, printer, drives, and mouse. If you are not sure what equipment you will be operating, check with your instructor. The computer system shown in Figure G.1 consists of six components. Each component is discussed separately in the material that follows.

Figure G.1 Microcomputer System

CPU

CPU stands for Central Processing Unit and it is the intelligence of the computer. All the processing occurs in the CPU. Silicon chips, which contain miniaturized circuitry, are placed on boards that are plugged into slots within the CPU. Whenever an instruction is given to the computer, that instruction is processed through circuitry in the CPU.

Monitor

The monitor is a piece of equipment that looks like a television screen. It displays the information of a program and the text being input at the keyboard. The quality of display for monitors varies depending on the type of monitor and the level of resolution. Monitors can also vary in size—generally from 14-inch size up to 21-inch size or larger.

Keyboard

The keyboard is used to input information into the computer. Keyboards for microcomputers vary in the number and location of the keys. Microcomputers have the alphabetic and numeric keys in the same location as the keys on a typewriter. The symbol keys, however, may be placed in a variety of locations, depending on the manufacturer. In addition to letters, numbers, and symbols, most microcomputer keyboards contain function keys, arrow keys, and a numeric keypad. Figure G.2 shows an enhanced keyboard.

Figure G.2 Keyboard

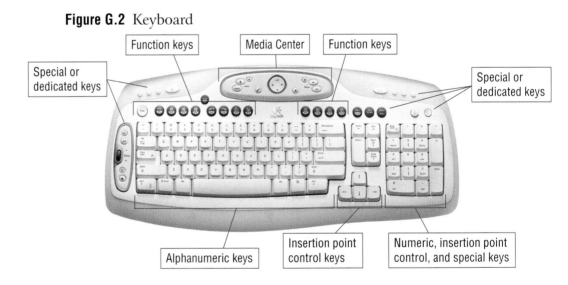

The 12 keys at the top of the keyboard, labeled with the letter F followed by a number, are called *function keys*. Use these keys to perform functions within each of the suite programs. To the right of the regular keys is a group of *special* or *dedicated keys*. These keys are labeled with specific functions that will be performed when you press the key. Below the special keys are arrow keys. Use these keys to move the insertion point in the document screen.

A keyboard generally includes three mode indicator lights. When you select certain modes, a light appears on the keyboard. For example, if you press the Caps Lock key, which disables the lowercase alphabet, a light appears next to Caps Lock. Similarly, pressing the Num Lock key will disable the special functions on the numeric keypad, which is located at the right side of the keyboard.

Disk Drives

Depending on the computer system you are using, Microsoft Office 2007 is installed on a hard drive or as part of a network system. Whether you are using Office on a hard drive or network system, you will need to have available a DVD or CD drive and a USB drive or other storage medium. You will insert the CD (compact disc) that accompanies this textbook in the DVD or CD drive and then copy folders from the CD to your storage medium. You will also save documents you complete at the computer to folders on your storage medium.

Printer

A document you create in Word is considered soft copy. If you want a hard copy of a document, you need to print it. To print documents you will need to access a printer, which will probably be either a laser printer or an ink-jet printer. A laser printer uses a laser beam combined with heat and pressure to print documents, while an ink-jet printer prints a document by spraying a fine mist of ink on the page.

Mouse

Many functions in the suite of programs are designed to operate more efficiently with a mouse. A mouse is an input device that sits on a flat surface next to the computer. You can operate a mouse with the left or the right hand. Moving the mouse on the flat surface causes a corresponding mouse pointer to move on the screen. Figure G.1 shows an illustration of a mouse.

Using the Mouse

The programs in the Microsoft Office suite can be operated using a keyboard or they can be operated with the keyboard and a mouse. The mouse may have two or three buttons on top, which are tapped to execute specific functions and commands. To use the mouse, rest it on a flat surface or a mouse pad. Put your hand over it with your palm resting on top of the mouse and your wrist resting on the table surface. As you move the mouse on the flat surface, a corresponding pointer moves on the screen.

When using the mouse, you should understand four terms—point, click, double-click, and drag. When operating the mouse, you may need to point to a specific command, button, or icon. Point means to position the mouse pointer on the desired item. With the mouse pointer positioned on the desired item, you may need to click a button on the mouse. Click means quickly tapping a button on the mouse once. To complete two steps at one time, such as choosing and then executing a function, double-click a mouse button. Double-click means to tap the left mouse button twice in quick succession. The term drag means to press and hold the left mouse button, move the mouse pointer to a specific location, and then release the button.

Using the Mouse Pointer

The mouse pointer will change appearance depending on the function being performed or where the pointer is positioned. The mouse pointer may appear as one of the following images:

- The mouse pointer appears as an I-beam (called the I-beam pointer) in the document screen and can be used to move the insertion point or select text.

- The mouse pointer appears as an arrow pointing up and to the left (called the arrow pointer) when it is moved to the Title bar, Quick Access toolbar, ribbon, or an option in a dialog box. For example, to open a new document with the mouse, position the I-beam pointer on the Office button located in the upper left corner of the screen until the pointer turns into an arrow pointer and then click the left mouse button. At the drop-down list that displays, make a selection by positioning the arrow pointer on the desired option and then clicking the left mouse button.

- The mouse pointer becomes a double-headed arrow (either pointing left and right, pointing up and down, or pointing diagonally) when performing certain functions such as changing the size of an object.

- In certain situations, such as moving an object or image, the mouse pointer displays with a four-headed arrow attached. The four-headed arrow means that you can move the object left, right, up, or down.

- When a request is being processed or when a program is being loaded, the mouse pointer may appear with a circle beside it. The moving circle means "please wait." When the process is completed, the circle is removed.

- The mouse pointer displays as a hand with a pointing index finger in certain functions such as Help and indicates that more information is available about the item.

Choosing Commands

Once a program is open, you can use several methods in the program to choose commands. A command is an instruction that tells the program to do something. You can choose a command using the mouse or the keyboard. When a program such as Word or PowerPoint is open, the ribbon contains buttons for completing tasks and contains tabs you click to display additional buttons. To choose a button on the Quick Access toolbar or in the ribbon, position the tip of the mouse arrow pointer on a button and then click the left mouse button.

The Office suite provides access keys you can press to use a command in a program. Press the Alt key on the keyboard to display KeyTips that identify the access key you need to press to execute a command. For example, press the Alt key in a Word document and KeyTips display as shown in Figure G.3. Continue pressing access keys until you execute the desired command. For example, if you want to begin spell checking a document, you would press the Alt key, press the R key on the keyboard to display the Review tab, and then press the letter S on the keyboard.

Figure G.3 Word KeyTips

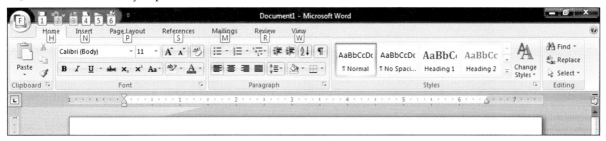

Choosing Commands from Drop-Down Lists

To choose a command from a drop-down list with the mouse, position the mouse pointer on the desired option and then click the left mouse button. To make a selection from a drop-down list with the keyboard, type the underlined letter in the desired option.

Some options at a drop-down list may be gray-shaded (dimmed), indicating that the option is currently unavailable. If an option at a drop-down list displays preceded by a check mark, that indicates that the option is currently active. If an option at a drop-down list displays followed by an ellipsis (...), a dialog box will display when that option is chosen.

Choosing Options from a Dialog Box

A dialog box contains options for applying formatting to a file or data within a file. Some dialog boxes display with tabs along the top providing additional options. For example, the Font dialog box shown in Figure G.4 contains two tabs—the Font tab and the Character Spacing tab. The tab that displays in the front is the

Figure G.4 Word Font Dialog Box

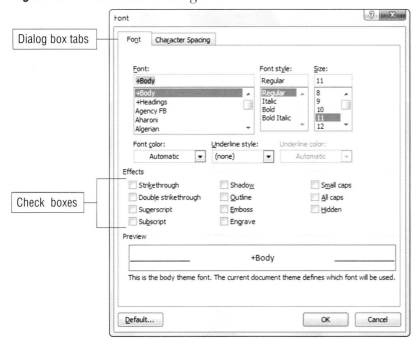

active tab. To make a tab active using the mouse, position the arrow pointer on the desired tab and then click the left mouse button. If you are using the keyboard, press Ctrl + Tab or press Alt + the underlined letter on the desired tab.

To choose options from a dialog box with the mouse, position the arrow pointer on the desired option and then click the left mouse button. If you are using the keyboard, press the Tab key to move the insertion point forward from option to option. Press Shift + Tab to move the insertion point backward from option to option. You can also hold down the Alt key and then press the underlined letter of the desired option. When an option is selected, it displays with a blue background or surrounded by a dashed box called a marquee. A dialog box contains one or more of the following elements: text boxes, list boxes, check boxes, option buttons, spin boxes, and command buttons.

Text Boxes

Some options in a dialog box require you to enter text. For example, the boxes below the *Find what* and *Replace with* options at the Excel Find and Replace dialog box shown in Figure G.5 are text boxes. In a text box, you type text or edit existing text. Edit text in a text box in the same manner as normal text. Use the Left and Right Arrow keys on the keyboard to move the insertion point without deleting text and use the Delete key or Backspace key to delete text.

Figure G.5 Excel Find and Replace Dialog Box

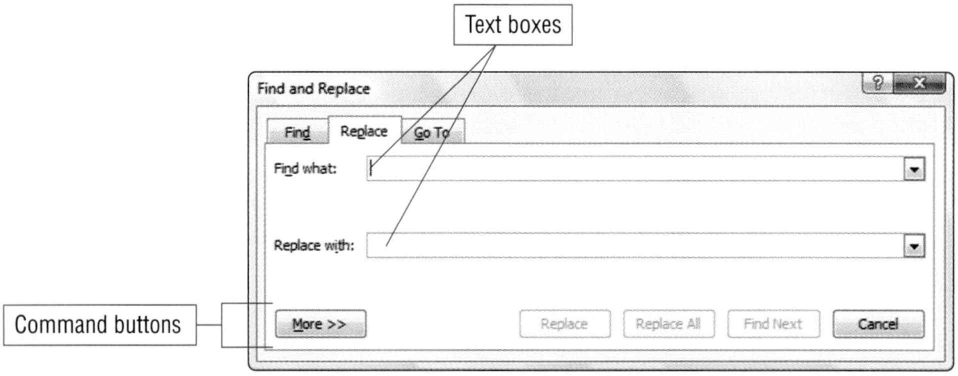

List Boxes

Some dialog boxes such as the Word Open dialog box shown in Figure G.6 may contain a list box. The list of files below the *Look in* option is contained in a list box. To make a selection from a list box with the mouse, move the arrow pointer to the desired option and then click the left mouse button.

Figure G.6 Word Open Dialog Box

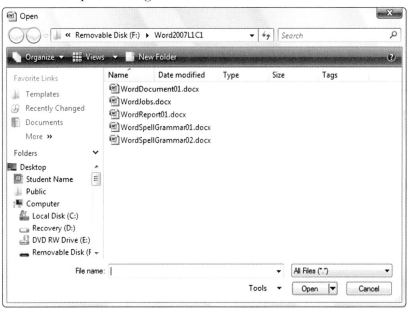

Some list boxes may contain a scroll bar. This scroll bar will display at the right side of the list box (a vertical scroll bar) or at the bottom of the list box (a horizontal scroll bar). You can use a vertical scroll bar or a horizontal scroll bar to move through the list if the list is longer than the box. To move down through a list on a vertical scroll bar, position the arrow pointer on the down-pointing arrow and hold down the left mouse button. To scroll up through the list in a vertical scroll bar, position the arrow pointer on the up-pointing arrow and hold down the left mouse button. You can also move the arrow pointer above the scroll box and click the left mouse button to scroll up the list or move the arrow pointer below the scroll box and click the left mouse button to move down the list. To move through a list with a horizontal scroll bar, click the left-pointing arrow to scroll to the left of the list or click the right-pointing arrow to scroll to the right of the list.

To make a selection from a list using the keyboard, move the insertion point into the box by holding down the Alt key and pressing the underlined letter of the desired option. Press the Up and/or Down Arrow keys on the keyboard to move through the list.

In some dialog boxes where enough room is not available for a list box, lists of options are inserted in a drop-down list box. Options that contain a drop-down list box display with a down-pointing arrow. For example, the *Underline style* option at the Word Font dialog box shown in Figure G.4 contains a drop-down list. To display the list, click the down-pointing arrow to the right of the *Underline style* option box. If you are using the keyboard, press Alt + U.

Check Boxes

Some dialog boxes contain options preceded by a box. A check mark may or may not appear in the box. The Word Font dialog box shown in Figure G.4 displays a variety of check boxes within the *Effects* section. If a check mark appears in the box, the option is active (turned on). If the check box does not contain a check mark, the option is inactive (turned off). Any number of check boxes can be active. For example, in the Word Font dialog box, you can insert a check mark in any or all of the boxes in the *Effects* section and these options will be active.

To make a check box active or inactive with the mouse, position the tip of the arrow pointer in the check box and then click the left mouse button. If you are using the keyboard, press Alt + the underlined letter of the desired option.

Option Buttons

The Word Print dialog box shown in Figure G.7 contains options in the *Print range* section preceded by option buttons. Only one option button can be selected at any time. When an option button is selected, a green circle displays in the button. To select an option button with the mouse, position the tip of the arrow pointer inside the option button and then click the left mouse button. To make a selection with the keyboard, hold down the Alt key and then press the underlined letter of the desired option.

Figure G.7 Word Print Dialog Box

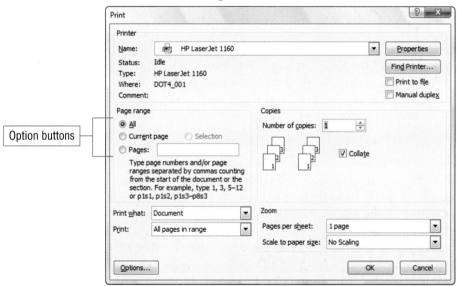

Option buttons

Spin Boxes

Some options in a dialog box contain measurements or numbers you can increase or decrease. These options are generally located in a spin box. For example, the Word Paragraph dialog box shown in Figure G.8 contains spin boxes located after the *Left*, *Right*, *Before*, and *After* options. To increase a number in a spin box, position the tip of the arrow pointer on the up-pointing arrow to the right of the desired option and then click the left mouse button. To decrease the number, click the down-pointing arrow. If you are using the keyboard, press Alt + the underlined letter of the desired option and then press the Up Arrow key to increase the number or the Down Arrow key to decrease the number.

Figure G.8 Word Paragraph Dialog Box

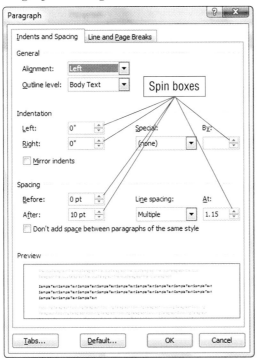

Command Buttons

In the Excel Find and Replace dialog box shown in Figure G.5, the boxes along the bottom of the dialog box are called command buttons. Use a command button to execute or cancel a command. Some command buttons display with an ellipsis (...). A command button that displays with an ellipsis will open another dialog box. To choose a command button with the mouse, position the arrow pointer on the desired button and then click the left mouse button. To choose a command button with the keyboard, press the Tab key until the desired command button contains the marquee and then press the Enter key.

Choosing Commands with Keyboard Shortcuts

Applications in the Office suite offer a variety of keyboard shortcuts you can use to executive specific commands. Keyboard shortcuts generally require two or more keys. For example, the keyboard shortcut to display the Open dialog box in an application is Ctrl + O. To use this keyboard shortcut, hold down the Ctrl key, type the letter O on the keyboard, and then release the Ctrl key. For a list of keyboard shortcuts, refer to the Help files.

Choosing Commands with Shortcut Menus

The software programs in the suite include menus that contain commands related to the item with which you are working. A shortcut menu appears in the file in the location where you are working. To display a shortcut menu, click the right mouse button or press Shift + F10. For example, if the insertion point is positioned in a paragraph of text in a Word document, clicking the right mouse button or pressing Shift + F10 will cause the shortcut menu shown in Figure G.9 to display in the document screen.

Figure G.9 Word Shortcut Menu

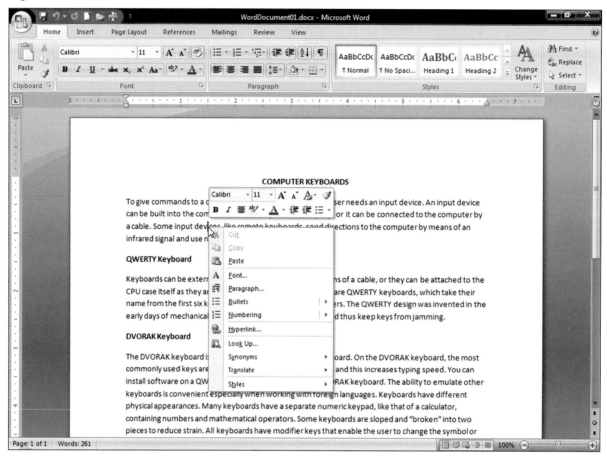

To select an option from a shortcut menu with the mouse, click the desired option. If you are using the keyboard, press the Up or Down Arrow key until the desired option is selected and then press the Enter key. To close a shortcut menu without choosing an option, click anywhere outside the shortcut menu or press the Esc key.

Working with Multiple Programs

As you learn the various programs in the Microsoft Office suite, you will notice how executing commands in each is very similar. For example, the steps to save, close, and print are virtually the same whether you are working in Word, Excel, or PowerPoint. This consistency between programs greatly enhances a user's ability to transfer knowledge learned in one program to another within the suite. Another appeal of Microsoft Office is the ability to have more than one program open at the same time. For example, you can open Word, create a document, and then open Excel, create a spreadsheet, and copy the spreadsheet into Word.

When you open a program, the name of the program displays in the Taskbar. If you open a file within the program, the file name follows the program name on the button on the Taskbar. If you open another program, the program name displays on a button positioned to the right of the first program button. Figure G.10 shows the Taskbar with Word, Excel, and PowerPoint open. To move from one program to another, click the button on the Taskbar representing the desired program file.

Figure G.10 Taskbar with Word, Excel, and PowerPoint Open

Completing Computer Projects

Some computer projects in this textbook require that you open an existing file. Project files are saved on the Student CD that accompanies this textbook. The files you need for each chapter are saved in individual folders. Before beginning a chapter, copy the necessary folder from the CD to your storage medium.

The Student CD also contains model answers in PDF format for the project exercises within (but not at the end of) each chapter so you can check your work. To access the PDF files, you will need to have Adobe Acrobat Reader installed on your computer's hard drive. A free download of Adobe Reader is available at Adobe Systems' Web site at www.adobe.com.

Copying a Folder

As you begin working in a chapter, copy the chapter folder from the CD to your storage medium (such as a USB flash drive) using the Computer window by completing the following steps:

1. Insert the CD that accompanies this textbook in the CD drive. At the AutoPlay window that displays, click the Close button located in the upper right corner of the window.
2. Insert your USB flash drive in an available USB port. If an AutoPlay window displays, click the Close button.
3. At the Windows Vista desktop, open the Computer window by clicking the Start button and then clicking *Computer* at the Start menu.
4. Double-click the CD drive in the Content pane (displays with the name *BMWord07StudentResources* preceded by the drive letter).
5. Double-click the desired program folder name in the Content pane.
6. Click once on the desired chapter subfolder name to select it.
7. Click the Organize button on the Command bar and then click *Copy* at the drop-down list.
8. In the *Folders* list box located at the left side of the Computer window, click the drive containing your storage medium.
9. Click the Organize button on the Command bar and then click *Paste* at the drop-down list.
10. Close the Computer window by clicking the Close button located in the upper right corner of the window.

Deleting a Folder

Note: Check with your instructor before deleting a folder. If storage capacity is an issue with your storage medium, delete any previous chapter folders before copying a chapter folder onto your storage medium. Delete a folder by completing the following steps:

1. Insert your storage medium (such as a USB flash drive) in the USB port.
2. At the Windows Vista desktop, open the Computer window by clicking the Start button and then clicking *Computer* at the Start menu.
3. Double-click the drive letter for your storage medium (drive containing your USB flash drive such as *Removable Disk (F:)*).
4. Click the chapter folder in the Content pane.
5. Click the Organize button on the Command bar and then click *Delete* at the drop-down list.
6. At the message asking if you want to delete the folder, click the Yes button.
7. Close the Computer window by clicking the Close button located in the upper right corner of the window.

Viewing or Printing the Project Model Answers

If you want to access the PDF model answer files, first make sure that Adobe Acrobat Reader is installed on your hard drive. Double-click the folder, double-click the desired chapter subfolder name, and double-click the appropriate file name to open the file. You can view and/or print the file to compare it with your own completed exercise file.

Customizing the Quick Access Toolbar

The four applications in the Office 2007 suite—Word, Excel, PowerPoint, and Access—each contain a Quick Access toolbar that displays at the top of the screen. By default, this toolbar contains three buttons: Save, Undo, and Redo. Before beginning chapters in this textbook, customize the Quick Access toolbar by adding three additional buttons: New, Open, and Quick Print. To add these three buttons to the Word Quick Access toolbar, complete the following steps:

1. Open Word.
2. Click the Customize Quick Access Toolbar button that displays at the right side of the toolbar.
3. At the drop-down list, click *New*. (This adds the New button to the toolbar.)
4. Click the Customize Quick Access Toolbar button and then click *Open* at the drop-down list. (This adds the Open button to the toolbar.)
5. Click the Customize Quick Access Toolbar button and then click *Quick Print* at the drop-down list. (This adds the Quick Print button to the toolbar.)

Complete the same steps for Excel, Access, and PowerPoint. You will only need to add the buttons once to the Quick Access toolbar. These buttons will remain on the toolbar even when you exit and then reopen the application.

Using Windows Vista

A computer requires an operating system to provide necessary instructions on a multitude of processes including loading programs, managing data, directing the flow of information to peripheral equipment, and displaying information. Windows Vista is an operating system that provides functions of this type (along with much more) in a graphical environment. Windows is referred to as a *graphical user interface* (GUI—pronounced *gooey*) that provides a visual display of information with features such as icons (pictures) and buttons. In this introduction, you will learn the basic features of Windows Vista:

Tutorial WV1
Exploring Windows Vista
Tutorial WV2
Working with Files and Folders
Tutorial WV3
Customizing Windows
Tutorial WV4
Using Gadgets and Applications

- Use desktop icons and the Taskbar to launch programs and open files or folders
- Organize and manage data, including copying, moving, creating, and deleting files and folders
- Personalize the desktop
- Use the Windows Help and Support Center features
- Customize monitor settings

Before using one of the software programs in the Microsoft Office suite, you will need to start the Windows Vista operating system. To do this, turn on the computer. Depending on your computer equipment configuration, you may also need to turn on the monitor and printer. If you are using a computer that is part of a network system or if your computer is set up for multiple users, a screen will display showing the user accounts defined for your computer system. At this screen, click your user account name and, if necessary, type your password and then press the Enter key. The Windows Vista operating system will start and, after a few moments, the desktop will display as shown in Figure W.1. (Your desktop may vary from what you see in Figure W.1.)

Figure W.1 Windows Vista Desktop

Icon

Sidebar

Start button

Taskbar

Exploring the Desktop

When Windows is loaded, the main portion of the screen is called the *desktop*. Think of the desktop in Windows as the top of a desk in an office. A business person places necessary tools—such as pencils, pens, paper, files, calculator—on the desktop to perform functions. Like the tools that are located on a desk, the desktop contains tools for operating the computer. These tools are logically grouped and placed in dialog boxes or panels that you can display using icons on the desktop. The desktop contains a variety of features for using your computer and software programs installed on the computer. The features available on the desktop are represented by icons and buttons.

Using Icons

Icons are visual symbols that represent programs, files, or folders. Figure W.1 identifies the *Recycle Bin* icon located on the Windows Vista desktop. The Windows Vista desktop on your computer may contain additional icons. Programs that have been installed on your computer may be represented by an icon on the desktop. Also, icons may display on your desktop representing files or folders. Double-click an icon and the program, file, or folder it represents opens on the desktop.

Adding and Closing Gadgets

The Sidebar at the right side of the Windows Vista desktop contains "gadgets," which are mini programs providing information at a glance and easy access to frequently used tools. Generally, the Sidebar contains the clock, calendar, and slide show gadgets, though the gadgets in your Sidebar may vary. To view the gadgets available, click the plus sign that displays at the top of the Sidebar. This displays the Gadget Gallery as shown in Figure W.2. To add a gadget to the Sidebar, double-click the desired gadget. To remove a gadget from the Sidebar, right-click the gadget and then click the *Close Gadget* option at the shortcut menu.

Figure W.2 Gadget Gallery

Using the Taskbar

The bar that displays at the bottom of the desktop (see Figure W.1) is called the Taskbar. The Taskbar, shown in Figure W.3, contains the Start button, the quick launch area, a section that displays task buttons representing open programs, and the notification area.

Figure W.3 Windows Vista Taskbar

Start button

Quick Launch toolbar

Taskbar

Notification area

Click the Start button, located at the left side of the Taskbar, and the Start menu displays as shown in Figure W.4 (your Start menu may vary). You can also display the Start menu by pressing the Windows key on your keyboard or by pressing Ctrl + Esc. The left side of the Start menu contains *pinned programs*, which are programs that always appear in that particular location on the Start menu, and links to the most recently and frequently used programs. The name of the currently logged on user displays at the top of the darker right portion of the menu followed by the user's personal folders. The two sections below the personal folders provide links to other Vista features, the Control Panel, and Windows Vista Help and Support. Use the buttons along the bottom right side of the Start menu to put the system in a power-conserving state, lock the computer, and shut down or put the computer in sleep mode.

Figure W.4 Start Menu

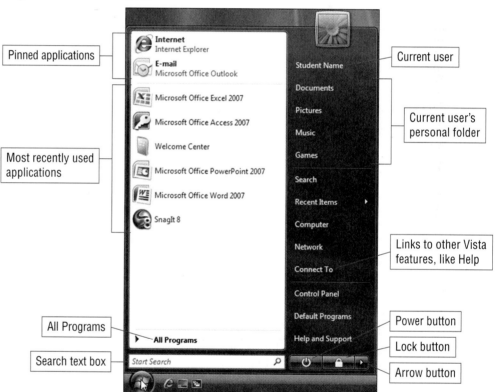

To choose an option from the Start menu, drag the arrow pointer to the desired option (referred to as *pointing*) and then click the left mouse button. Pointing to options at the Start menu that are followed by a right-pointing arrow will cause a side menu to display with additional options. When a program is open, a task button representing the program appears on the Taskbar. If multiple programs are open, each program will appear as a task button on the Taskbar (a few specialized tools may not).

Project ① Opening Programs and Switching between Programs

1. Open Windows Vista. (To do this, turn on the computer and, if necessary, turn on the monitor and/or printer. If you are using a computer that is part of a network system or if your computer is set up for multiple users, you may need to click your user account name and, if necessary, type your password and then press the Enter key. Check with your instructor to determine if you need to complete any additional steps.)
2. When the Windows Vista desktop displays, add and close a gadget in the Sidebar by completing the following steps:
   a. Click the plus sign that displays at the top of the Sidebar. (This displays the Gadget Gallery.)

Step 2a

Step 2b

   b. At the Gadget Gallery, double-click the Weather gadget.
   c. Close the Gadget Gallery by clicking the Close button that displays in the upper right corner of the window.
   d. Position the mouse pointer on the Weather gadget (this displays icons at the right side of the icon) and then click the search icon that displays with a magnifying glass.

Step 2d

   e. At the Weather dialog box that displays, type your city name, type a comma, type your two-letter state abbreviation, and then press the Enter key.
   f. Click OK to close the dialog box. (Notice that the Weather gadget displays the current temperature for your city.)
   g. Close the Weather gadget by positioning the mouse pointer on the Weather gadget and then clicking the right mouse button.

Step 2g

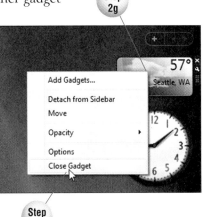

   h. At the shortcut menu that displays, click the *Close Gadget* option.

Step 2h

3. At the Windows Vista desktop, open Microsoft Word by completing the following steps:
   a. Position the arrow pointer on the Start button on the Taskbar and then click the left mouse button.
   b. At the Start menu, point to *All Programs* (a side menu displays) and then click *Microsoft Office* (this displays programs in the Office suite below Microsoft Office).
   c. Drag the arrow pointer down to *Microsoft Office Word 2007* and then click the left mouse button.

d. When the Microsoft Word program is open, notice that a task button representing Word displays on the Taskbar.

Step
3d

4. Open Microsoft Excel by completing the following steps:
   a. Position the arrow pointer on the Start button on the Taskbar and then click the left mouse button.
   b. At the Start menu, point to *All Programs* and then click *Microsoft Office*.
   c. Drag the arrow pointer down to *Microsoft Office Excel 2007* and then click the left mouse button.
   d. When the Microsoft Excel program is open, notice that a task button representing Excel displays on the Taskbar to the right of the task button representing Word.
5. Switch to the Word program by clicking the task button on the Taskbar representing Word.

Step
5

Step
7

6. Switch to the Excel program by clicking the task button on the Taskbar representing Excel.
7. Exit Excel by clicking the Close button that displays in the upper right corner of the Excel window.
8. Exit Word by clicking the Close button that displays in the upper right corner of the Word window.

Using the Quick Launch Toolbar

The Quick Launch toolbar displays on the Taskbar just right of the Start button (see Figure W.3) and includes shortcuts to frequently used programs. To open a program, click the icon on the Quick Launch toolbar representing the desired program. To add a program icon to the toolbar, click the desired program icon and then drag it to the Quick Launch toolbar. To remove a program icon from the toolbar, right-click the icon and then click *Close* at the shortcut menu. At the message that displays asking if you want to move the shortcut to the Recycle Bin, click Yes.

Exploring the Notification Area

The notification area is located at the right side of the Taskbar and contains the system clock along with small icons representing programs that run in the background. Position the arrow pointer over the current time in the notification area of the Taskbar and today's date displays in a box above the time. Click the time in the notification area and a window displays with the current date, a calendar of the current month, and a clock with the current time. Click the *Change date and time settings* text that displays at the bottom of the window and the Date and Time dialog box displays. To change the date and/or time, click the Change date and time button and the Date and Time Settings dialog box displays similar to the dialog box shown in Figure W.5. (If a dialog box displays telling you that Windows needs your permission to continue, click the Continue button.)

Figure W.5 Date and Time Settings Dialog Box

Change the month and year by clicking the left-pointing or right-pointing arrow at the top of the calendar in the *Date* section. Click the left-pointing arrow to display the previous month(s) and click the right-pointing arrow to display the next month(s).

To change the day, click the desired day in the monthly calendar that displays in the dialog box. To change the time, double-click either the hour, minute, or seconds and then type the appropriate time or use the up- and down-pointing arrows to adjust the time.

Some programs, when installed, will add an icon to the notification area of the Taskbar. Display the name of the icon by positioning the mouse pointer on the icon and, after approximately one second, the icon label displays. If more icons have been inserted in the notification area than can be viewed at one time, a left-pointing arrow button displays at the left side of the notification area. Click this left-pointing arrow button and the remaining icons display.

Setting Taskbar Properties

You can customize the Taskbar with options from the Taskbar shortcut menu. Display this menu by right-clicking on an empty portion of the Taskbar. The Taskbar shortcut menu shown in Figure W.6 contains options for turning on or off the display of specific toolbars, specifying the display of multiple windows, displaying the Windows Task Manager dialog box, locking or unlocking the Taskbar, and displaying the Taskbar and Start Menu Properties dialog box.

Figure W.6 Taskbar Shortcut Menu

With options in the Taskbar and Start Menu Properties dialog box shown in Figure W.7, you can change settings for the Taskbar as well as the Start menu. Display this dialog box by right-clicking on an empty space on the Taskbar and then clicking *Properties* at the shortcut menu.

Figure W.7 Taskbar and Start Menu Properties Dialog Box

Each property is controlled by a check box. Property options containing a check mark are active. Click the option to remove the check mark and make the option inactive. If an option is inactive, clicking the option will insert a check mark in the check box and turn on the option (make it active).

Project ② Changing Taskbar Properties

1. Make sure the Windows Vista desktop displays.
2. Hide the Taskbar and remove the display of the Quick Launch toolbar by completing the following steps:
   a. Position the arrow pointer on any empty area on the Taskbar and then click the right mouse button.
   b. At the shortcut menu that displays, click *Properties*.
   c. At the Taskbar and Start Menu Properties dialog box, click *Auto-hide the taskbar*. (This inserts a check mark in the check box.)
   d. Click *Show Quick Launch*. (This removes the check mark from the check box.)
   e. Click the Apply button.
   f. Click OK to close the dialog box.
3. Display the Taskbar by positioning the mouse pointer at the bottom of the screen. When the Taskbar displays, notice that the Quick Launch toolbar no longer displays on the Taskbar.
4. Return to the default settings for the Taskbar by completing the following steps:
   a. With the Taskbar displayed (if it does not display, position the mouse pointer at the bottom of the desktop), position the arrow pointer on any empty area on the Taskbar and then click the right mouse button.
   b. At the shortcut menu that displays, click *Properties*.
   c. At the Taskbar and Start Menu Properties dialog box, click *Auto-hide the taskbar*. (This removes the check mark from the check box.)
   d. Click *Show Quick Launch*. (This inserts a check mark in the check box.)
   e. Click the Apply button.
   f. Click OK to close the dialog box.

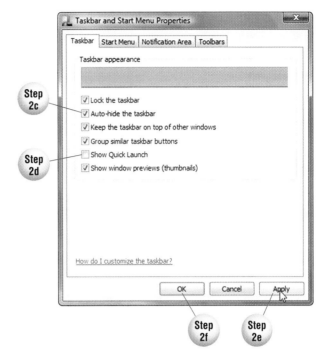

Step 2c
Step 2d
Step 2f
Step 2e

Powering Down the Computer

Windows Vista offers a variety of methods for powering down your computer. You can put the computer into sleep mode or hibernate mode, lock the system without turning it off, log off, restart the computer, or shut down the computer.

Use the sleep mode if you want to save power without having to close all files and applications. To put the computer to sleep, click the Start button and then click the Power button that displays toward the lower right corner of the Start menu (refer to Figure W.8). In sleep mode, Vista saves files and information about open programs and then powers down the computer to a low-power state. To "wake" the computer back up, quickly press the computer's power button.

Figure W.8 Power Button

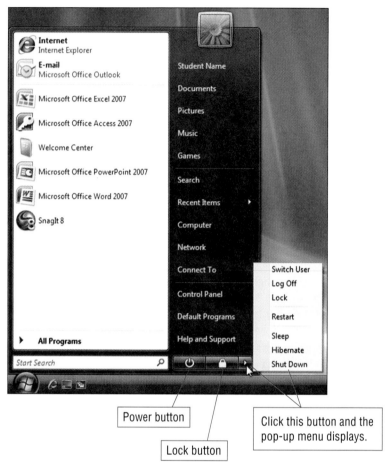

Power button

Lock button

Click this button and the pop-up menu displays.

You can put your computer in hibernate mode, which saves your work session and shuts down the computer. When you restart your computer, the files and programs are open on the desktop. To put the computer in hibernate mode, click the Start button and then click the button containing a right-pointing triangle that displays in the lower right corner of the Start menu. At the pop-up menu that displays, click the *Hibernate* option.

If you need to walk away from your computer and you want to protect your work, consider locking the computer. When you lock the computer, the desktop is hidden but the system is not shut down and the power is not conserved. To lock the computer, click the Start button and then click the lock button that displays in the lower right corner of the Start menu. To unlock the computer, click the icon on the desktop representing your account, type your password, and then press Enter.

In a multi-user environment you can log off your computer, which shuts down your applications and files and makes system resources available to other users logged on to the system. To log off, click the Start button and then click the button containing the right-pointing arrow (located in the lower right corner of the Start menu). At the pop-up menu that displays, click *Log Off*.

If you want to shut down Windows Vista and turn off all power to the computer, shut down the computer. To do this, click the Start button and then click the button containing the right-pointing triangle. At the pop-up menu that displays, click *Shut Down*.

Managing Files and Folders

As you begin working with programs in Windows Vista, you will create files in which data (information) is saved. A file might contain a Word document, an Excel workbook, or a PowerPoint presentation. As you begin creating files, consider creating folders into which those files will be stored. You can complete file management tasks such as creating a folder and copying and moving files and folders at the Computer window. To display the Computer window shown in Figure W.9, click the Start button on the Taskbar and then click *Computer*. The various components of the Computer window are identified in Figure W.9.

Figure W.9 Computer Window

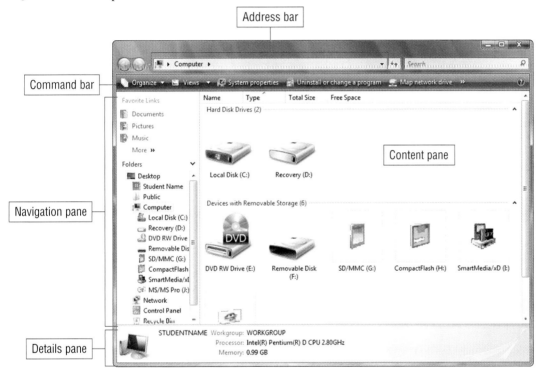

Copying, Moving, and Deleting Files and Folders

File and folder management activities might include copying and moving files or folders from one folder or drive to another, or deleting files or folders. The Computer window offers a variety of methods for copying, moving, and deleting files and folders. This section will provide you with steps for copying, moving, and deleting files and folders using options from the Organize button on the Command bar and the shortcut menu.

To copy a file to another folder or drive, first display the file in the Content pane by identifying the location of the file. If the file is located in the Documents folder, click the *Documents* folder in the *Favorite Links* list box in the Navigation pane or click the *Documents* folder in the *Folders* list box. If the file is located on the hard drive or other storage medium, click the desired location in the *Folders* list box in the Navigation pane. Next, click the file name in the Content pane that you want to copy, click the Organize button on the Command bar, and then click *Copy* at the drop-down list. In the *Folders* list box, click the location where you want to copy the file. Click the Organize button and then click *Paste* at the drop-down list. You would complete similar steps to copy and paste a folder to another location.

To move a file, click the desired file in the Content pane, click the Organize button on the Command bar, and then click *Cut* at the drop-down list. Navigate to the desired location, click the Organize button, and then click *Paste* at the drop-down list.

To delete a file(s) or folder(s), click the file or folder in the Content pane in the Computer window or select multiple files or folders. Click the Organize button on the Command bar and then click *Delete* at the drop-down list. At the message asking if you want to move the file or folder to the Recycle Bin, click the Yes button.

In Project 3, you will insert the CD that accompanies this book into the DVD or CD drive. When the CD is inserted, the drive may automatically activate and a dialog box may display telling you that the disk or device contains more than one type of content and asking what you want Windows to do. If this dialog box displays, click the Cancel button.

Project ③   Copying a File and Folder and Deleting a File

1. Insert the CD that accompanies this textbook into the appropriate drive. If a dialog box displays telling you that the disk or device contains more than one type of content and asking what you want Windows to do, click the Cancel button.
2. Insert your storage medium (such as a USB flash drive) in the USB port (or other drive).
3. At the Windows Vista desktop, click the Start button and then click *Computer* located at the right side of the Start menu.
4. Copy a file from the CD that accompanies this textbook to the drive containing your storage medium by completing the following steps:
   a. Double-click the CD drive in the Content pane containing the CD from the book.
   b. Double-click the *StudentDataFiles* folder in the Content pane.
   c. Double-click the *WindowsVista* folder in the Content pane.
   d. Click **WordDocument01.docx** in the Content pane.
   e. Click the Organize button on the Command bar and then click *Copy* at the drop-down list.
   f. In the Folders list box in the Navigation pane, click the drive containing your storage medium. (You may need to scroll down the list box.)
   g. Click the Organize button on the Command bar and then click *Paste* at the drop-down list.

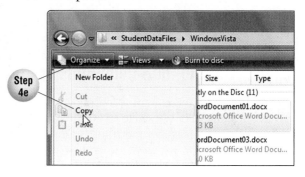

5. Delete **WordDocument01.docx** from your storage medium by completing the following steps:
   a. Make sure the contents of your storage medium display in the Content pane in the Computer window.
   b. Click **WordDocument01.docx** in the Content pane to select it.

c. Click the Organize button on the Command bar and then click *Delete* at the drop-down list.

d. At the message asking if you want to delete the file, click the Yes button.

6. Copy the WindowsVista folder from the CD to your storage medium by completing the following steps:

a. With the Computer window open, click the drive in the *Folders* list box in the Navigation pane that contains the CD that accompanies this book.

b. Double-click *StudentDataFiles* in the Content pane.

c. Click the *WindowsVista* folder in the Content pane.

d. Click the Organize button on the Command bar and then click *Copy* at the drop-down list.

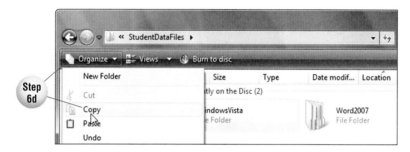

e. In the *Folders* list box in the Navigation pane in the Computer window, click the drive containing your storage medium.

f. Click the Organize button on the Command bar and then click *Paste* at the drop-down list.

7. Close the Computer window by clicking the Close button located in the upper right corner of the window.

In addition to options in the Organize button drop-down list, you can use options in a shortcut menu to copy, move, and delete files or folders. To use a shortcut menu, select the desired file(s) or folder(s), position the mouse pointer on the selected item, and then click the right mouse button. At the shortcut menu that displays, click the desired option such as Copy, Cut, or Delete.

Selecting Files and Folders

You can move, copy, or delete more than one file or folder at the same time. Before moving, copying, or deleting files or folders, select the desired files or folders. To make selecting easier, consider changing the display in the Content pane to List or Details. To change the display, click the Views button arrow on the Command bar in the Computer window and then click *List* or *Details* at the drop-down list.

To select adjacent files or folders, click the first file or folder, hold down the Shift key, and then click the last file or folder. To select nonadjacent files or folders, click the first file or folder, hold down the Ctrl key, and then click any other files or folders.

Project ④ Copying and Deleting Files

1. At the Windows Vista desktop, click the Start button and then click *Computer*.
2. Copy files from the CD that accompanies this textbook to the drive containing your storage medium by completing the following steps:

   a. Make sure the CD that accompanies this textbook and your storage medium are inserted in the appropriate drives.

   b. Double-click the CD drive in the Content pane in the Computer window.

   c. Double-click the *StudentDataFiles* folder in the Content pane.

   d. Double-click the *WindowsVista* folder in the Content pane.

   e. Change the display to Details by clicking the Views button arrow on the Command bar and then clicking *Details* at the drop-down list.

   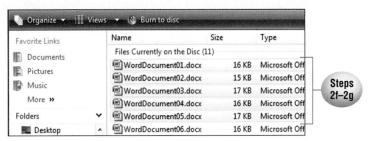

   f. Click **WordDocument01.docx** in the Content pane.

   g. Hold down the Shift key, click **WordDocument05.docx**, and then release the Shift key. (This selects five documents.)

   h. Click the Organize button on the Command bar and then click *Copy* at the drop-down list.

   i. In the *Folders* list box located at the left side of the Computer window, click the drive containing your storage medium.

   j. Click the Organize button on the Command bar and then click *Paste* at the drop-down list.

3. Delete the files from your storage medium that you just copied by completing the following steps:

   a. Change the view by clicking the Views button arrow on the Command bar and then clicking *List* at the drop-down list.

   b. Click **WordDocument01.docx** in the Content pane.

   c. Hold down the Shift key, click **WordDocument05.docx**, and then release the Shift key.

   d. Position the mouse pointer on any selected file, click the right mouse button, and then click *Delete* at the shortcut menu.

   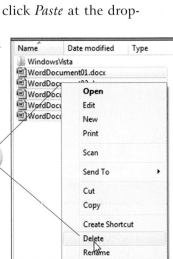

   e. At the message asking if you are sure you want to move the files to the Recycle Bin, click Yes.

4. Close the Computer window by clicking the Close button located in the upper right corner of the window.

Manipulating and Creating Folders

As you begin working with and creating a number of files, consider creating folders in which you can logically group the files. To create a folder, display the Computer window and then display in the Content pane the drive or folder where you want to create the folder. Position the mouse pointer in a blank area in the Content pane, click the right mouse button, point to *New* in the shortcut menu, and then click *Folder* at the side menu. This inserts a folder icon in the Content pane and names the folder *New Folder*. Type the desired name for the new folder and then press Enter.

Project ⑤ Creating a New Folder

1. At the Windows Vista desktop, open the Computer window.
2. Create a new folder by completing the following steps:
   a. Double-click in the Content pane the drive that contains your storage medium.
   b. Double-click the *WindowsVista* folder in the Content pane. (This opens the folder.)
   c. Position the mouse pointer in a blank area in the Content pane and then click the right mouse button.
   d. Point to *New* in the shortcut menu and then click *Folder* at the side menu.

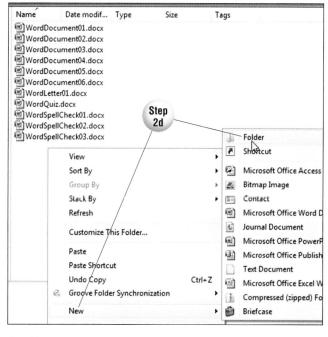

   e. Type SpellCheckFiles and then press Enter. (This changes the name from *New Folder* to *SpellCheckFiles*.)
3. Copy **WordSpellCheck01.docx**, **WordSpellCheck02.docx**, and **WordSpellCheck03.docx** into the SpellCheckFiles folder you just created by completing the following steps:
   a. Click the Views button arrow on the Command bar and then click *List* at the drop-down list. (Skip this step if *List* is already selected.)
   b. Click once on the file named **WordSpellCheck01.docx** located in the Content pane.

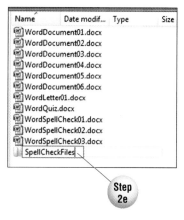

c. Hold down the Shift key, click once on the file named **WordSpellCheck03.docx**, and then release the Shift key. (This selects three documents.)

d. Click the Organize button on the Command bar and then click *Copy* at the drop-down list.

e. Double-click the *SpellCheckFiles* folder in the Content pane.

f. Click the Organize button on the Command bar and then click *Paste* at the drop-down list.

4. Delete the SpellCheckFiles folder and its contents by completing the following steps:

a. Click the Back button (contains a left-pointing arrow) located at the left side of the Address bar.

b. Click the *SpellCheckFiles* folder in the Content pane to select it.

c. Click the Organize button on the Command bar and then click *Delete* at the drop-down list.

d. At the message asking you to confirm the deletion, click Yes.

5. Close the window by clicking the Close button located in the upper right corner of the window.

Using the Recycle Bin

Deleting the wrong file can be a disaster but Windows Vista helps protect your work with the Recycle Bin. The Recycle Bin acts just like an office wastepaper basket; you can "throw away" (delete) unwanted files, but you can "reach in" to the Recycle Bin and take out (restore) a file if you threw it away by accident.

Deleting Files to the Recycle Bin

A file or folder or selected files or folders you delete from the hard drive are sent automatically to the Recycle Bin. If you want to permanently delete files or folders from the hard drive without first sending them to the Recycle Bin, select the desired file(s) or folder(s), right click on one of the selected files or folders, hold down the Shift key, and then click *Delete* at the shortcut menu.

Files and folders deleted from a USB flash drive or disk are deleted permanently. (Recovery programs are available, however, that will help you recover deleted text. If you accidentally delete a file or folder from a USB flash drive or disk, do not do anything more with the USB flash drive or disk until you can run a recovery program.)

You can delete files in the manner described earlier in this section and you can also delete a file by dragging the file icon to the Recycle Bin. To do this, click the desired file in the Content pane in the Computer window, drag the file icon on top of the Recycle Bin icon on the desktop until the text *Move to Recycle Bin* displays, and then release the mouse button.

Restoring Files from the Recycle Bin

To restore a file from the Recycle Bin, double-click the *Recycle Bin* icon on the desktop. This opens the Recycle Bin window shown in Figure W.10. (The contents of the Recycle Bin will vary.) To restore a file, click the file you want restored and then click the Restore this item button on the Command bar. This removes the file from the Recycle Bin and returns it to its original location. You can also restore a file by positioning the mouse pointer on the file, clicking the right mouse button, and then clicking *Restore* at the shortcut menu.

Figure W.10 Recycle Bin Window

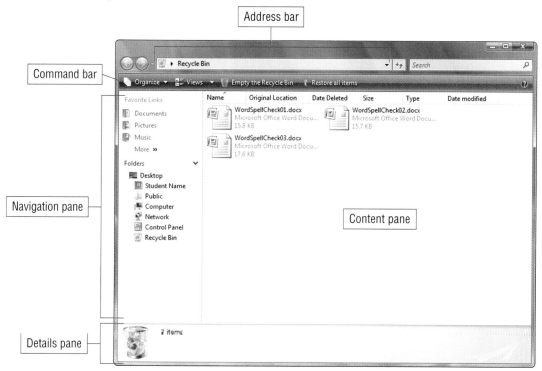

Project ⑥ Deleting Files to and Restoring Files from the Recycle Bin

Before beginning this project, check with your instructor to determine if you can copy files to the hard drive.

1. At the Windows Vista desktop, open the Computer window.
2. Copy files from your storage medium to the Documents folder on your hard drive by completing the following steps:
   a. Double-click in the Content pane the drive containing your storage medium.
   b. Double-click the *WindowsVista* folder in the Content pane.
   c. Click the Views button arrow on the Command bar and then click *List* at the drop-down list. (Skip this step if *List* is already selected.)
   d. Click **WordSpellCheck01.docx** in the Content pane.
   e. Hold down the Shift key, click **WordSpellCheck03.docx**, and then release the Shift key.
   f. Click the Organize button on the Command bar and then click *Copy* at the drop-down list.

g. Click the *Documents* folder in the *Favorite Links* list box in the Navigation pane.

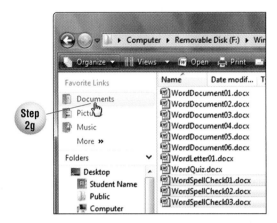

h. Click the Organize button on the Command bar and then click *Paste* at the drop-down list.
3. Delete to the Recycle Bin the files you just copied by completing the following steps:
   a. Select **WordSpellCheck01.docx** through **WordSpellCheck03.docx** in the Content pane. (If the files are not visible, you will need to scroll down the list of files in the Content pane.)
   b. Click the Organize button on the Command bar and then click *Delete* at the drop-down list.
   c. At the message asking you if you are sure you want to move the items to the Recycle Bin, click Yes.
4. Close the Computer window.
5. At the Windows Vista desktop, display the contents of the Recycle Bin by double-clicking the Recycle Bin icon.
6. Restore the files you just deleted by completing the following steps:
   a. Select **WordSpellCheck01.docx** through **WordSpellCheck03.docx** in the Recycle Bin Content pane. (If these files are not visible, you will need to scroll down the list of files in the Content pane.)
   b. Click the Restore the selected items button on the Command bar.

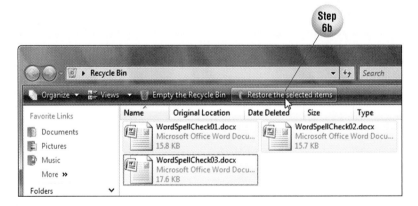

7. Close the Recycle Bin by clicking the Close button located in the upper right corner of the window.
8. Display the Computer window.
9. Click the *Documents* folder in the *Favorite Links* list box in the Navigation pane.
10. Delete the files you restored.
11. Close the Computer window.

Emptying the Recycle Bin

Just like a wastepaper basket, the Recycle Bin can get full. To empty the Recycle Bin, position the arrow pointer on the *Recycle Bin* icon on the desktop and then click the right mouse button. At the shortcut menu that displays, click the *Empty Recycle Bin* option. At the message asking if you want to permanently delete the items, click Yes. You can also empty the Recycle Bin by displaying the Recycle Bin window and then clicking the Empty the Recycle Bin button on the Command bar. At the message asking if you want to permanently delete the items, click Yes. To delete a specific file from the Recycle Bin window, click the desired file in the Recycle Bin window, click the Organize button, and then *Delete* at the drop-down list. At the message asking if you want to permanently delete the file, click Yes. When you empty the Recycle Bin, the files cannot be recovered by the Recycle Bin or by Windows Vista. If you have to recover a file, you will need to use a file recovery program.

Project ⑦   Emptying the Recycle Bin

Before beginning this project, check with your instructor to determine if you can delete files/folders from the Recycle Bin.

1. At the Windows Vista desktop, double-click the *Recycle Bin* icon.
2. At the Recycle Bin window, empty the contents by clicking the Empty the Recycle Bin button on the Command bar.
3. At the message asking you if you want to permanently delete the items, click Yes.
4. Close the Recycle Bin by clicking the Close button located in the upper right corner of the window.

Creating a Shortcut

If you use a file or program on a consistent basis, consider creating a shortcut to the file or program. A shortcut is a specialized icon that represents very small files that point the operating system to the actual item, whether it is a file, a folder, or an application. If you create a shortcut to a Word document, the shortcut icon is not the actual document but a path to the document. Double-click the shortcut icon and Windows Vista opens the document in Word.

One method for creating a shortcut is to display the Computer window and then make active the drive or folder where the file is located. Right-click the desired file, point to *Send To*, and then click *Desktop (create shortcut)*. You can easily delete a shortcut icon from the desktop by dragging the shortcut icon to the Recycle Bin icon. This deletes the shortcut icon but does not delete the file to which the shortcut pointed.

Project ⑧ Creating a Shortcut

1. At the Windows Vista desktop, display the Computer window.
2. Double-click the drive containing your storage medium.
3. Double-click the *WindowsVista* folder in the Content pane.
4. Change the display of files to a list by clicking the Views button arrow on the Command bar and then clicking *List* at the drop-down list. (Skip this step if *List* is already selected.)
5. Create a shortcut to the file named **WordLetter01.docx** by right-clicking **WordLetter01.docx**, pointing to *Send To*, and then clicking *Desktop (create shortcut)*.

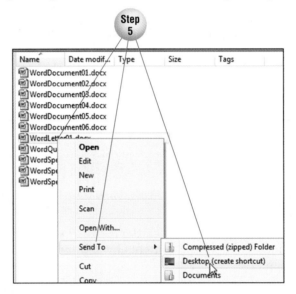

Step 5

6. Close the Computer window.
7. Open Word and the file named **WordLetter01.docx** by double-clicking the *WordLetter01.docx* shortcut icon on the desktop.
8. After viewing the file in Word, exit Word by clicking the Close button that displays in the upper right corner of the window.
9. Delete the *WordLetter01.docx* shortcut icon by completing the following steps:
   a. At the desktop, position the mouse pointer on the *WordLetter01.docx* shortcut icon.
   b. Hold down the left mouse button, drag the icon on top of the *Recycle Bin* icon, and then release the mouse button.

Step 7

Personalizing Appearances and Sounds

You can personalize the appearance of and the sounds on your computer to fit your particular needs and preferences. Use options in the Personalization window shown in Figure W.11 to make personalization choices. Display this window by right-clicking in a blank area on the desktop and then clicking *Personalize* at the shortcut menu.

Figure W.11 Personalization Window

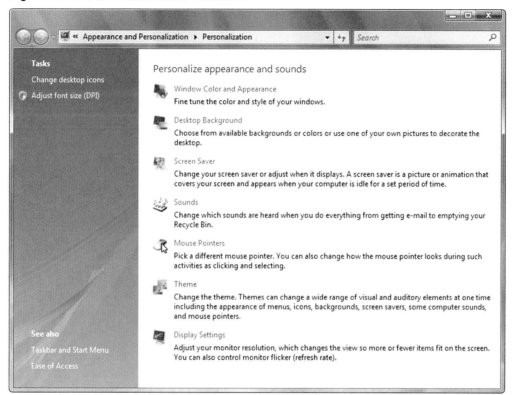

At the Personalization window, a description displays below each option. For example, the description "Fine tune the color and style of your windows." displays below the *Window Color and Appearance* option. Click the option and the window displays with color and color intensity choices. With the other options, you can change the desktop background; add a screen saver; and change sounds, mouse pointers, themes, and display settings.

Project ⑨   Personalizing the Desktop and Mouse Pointer

1. At the Windows Vista desktop, right-click in a blank area on the desktop and then click *Personalize* at the shortcut menu.
2. At the Personalization window, click the *Window Color and Appearance* option.
3. Click the *Red* option in the *Window Color and Appearance* section. (This changes the border of the window and the border of dialog boxes to red.)

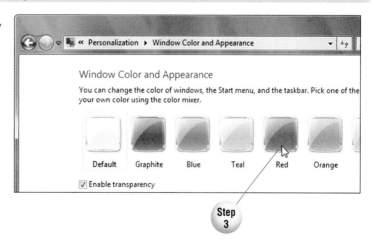

Step 3

4. Click OK to close the Window Color and Appearance window.
5. Click the *Desktop Background* option.
6. At the Desktop Background window, scroll through the list of pictures and then locate the currently selected picture. (The selected picture will display surrounded by a light gray border and border line. The default picture file name is probably *img24.jpg*.)
7. Click the **img20.jpg** image in the list box (see image at right). (To display the file name of the picture, hover the mouse pointer over the picture.)
8. Click the option at the right (Center) in the *How should the picture be positioned?* section.

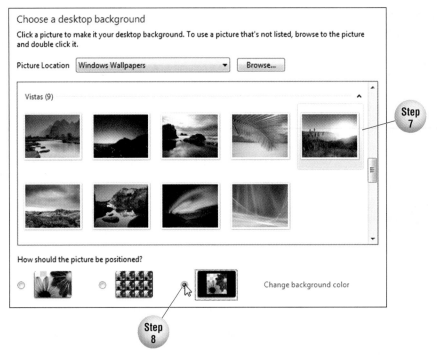

9. Click OK to close the window. (Notice that the desktop picture changes to reflect your choice and the picture is centered.)
10. Click the *Screen Saver* option in the Personalization window.
11. At the Screen Saver Settings dialog box, click the *Screen saver* option box and then click *Aurora* at the drop-down list.
12. Click the down-pointing arrow at the right side of the *Wait* option box until *1* displays in the box.
13. Click OK to close the dialog box.
14. Click the *Sounds* option in the Personalization window, notice the options that display in the Sound dialog box, and then click Cancel to close the dialog box.
15. Click the *Mouse Pointers* option in the Personalization window.
16. At the Mouse Properties dialog box, click each tab and notice the options that display.

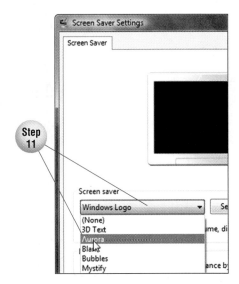

17. Click the Pointer Options tab.
18. Click the *Display pointer trails* check box in the *Visibility* section to insert a check mark.
19. Drag the button on the slider bar approximately to the middle of the bar.

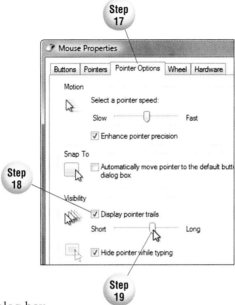

20. Click OK to close the dialog box.
21. Click the *Theme* option in the Personalization window.
22. At the Theme Settings dialog box, click the *Theme* option box and then notice the theme options at the drop-down list.
23. Click Cancel to close the dialog box.
24. Click the *Display Settings* option in the Personalization window.
25. At the Display Settings dialog box, notice the options in the dialog box and then click the Cancel button.
26. Close the Personalization window.
27. Let the computer sit idle for over a minute (do not move the mouse) until the screen saver displays on the screen.
28. After viewing the screen saver, return the personalization settings back to the default by completing the following steps:
    a. Display the Personalization window by right-clicking in a blank area on the Windows Vista desktop and then clicking *Personalize* at the shortcut menu.
    b. At the Personalization window, click the *Window Color and Appearance* option.
    c. Click the *Default* option in the *Window Color and Appearance* section.

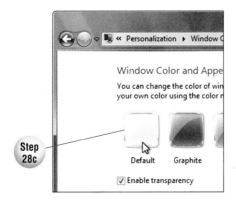

d. Click OK to close the Window Color and Appearance window.
e. Click the *Desktop Background* option.
f. At the Desktop Background window, scroll through the list of pictures and then click the default picture (probably *img24.jpg*).
g. Click the option at the left (Fit to screen) in the *How should the picture be positioned?* section.

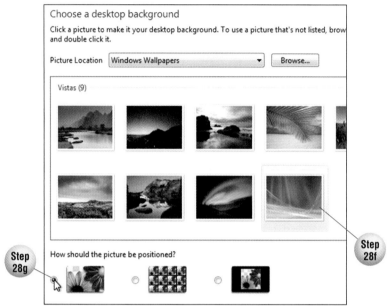

Step 28f

Step 28g

h. Click OK to close the window.
i. Click the Screen Saver option in the Personalization window.
j. At the Screen Saver Settings dialog box, click the *Screen saver* option box and then click *Windows Logo* at the drop-down list.
k. Click the up-pointing arrow at the right side of the *Wait* option box until *3* displays in the box.
l. Click OK to close the dialog box.
m. Click the *Mouse Pointers* option in the Personalization window.
n. At the Mouse Properties dialog box, click the Pointer Options tab.
o. Click the *Display pointer trails* check box in the *Visibility* section to remove the check mark.
p. Click OK to close the dialog box.
29. Close the Personalization window.

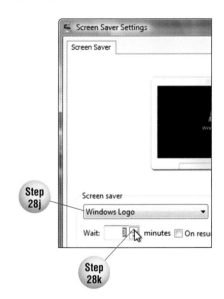

Step 28j

Step 28k

Exploring Windows Vista Help and Support

Windows Vista includes an on-screen reference guide providing information, explanations, and interactive help on learning Windows features. Use options in the Windows Help and Support window shown in Figure W.12 to get assistance on Windows features.

Figure W.12 Windows Help and Support Window

Use options in the *Find an answer* section to display information on Windows basics, security and maintenance, and access the Windows online help. You can also use options in this section to display a table of contents of help features, access troubleshooting information, and display information on what's new in Windows Vista. The Windows Help and Support window includes a Command bar that includes buttons to display the opening Windows Help and Support window, print the current information in the Help window, display a table of contents of Windows Vista features, get customer support or other types of services, and display a list of Help options.

Project ⑩ Using Windows Help and Support

1. At the Windows Vista desktop, click the Start button and then click *Help and Support* at the Start menu.
2. At the Windows Help and Support window, click the *Windows Basic* option in the *Find an answer* section.
3. At the information that displays in the Help window, click a topic that interests you and then read the information.
4. Click the Back button located at the left side of the Command bar to display the previous window.

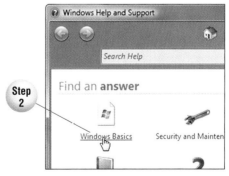

Step 2

Step 4

5. Click another topic that interests you and then read the information.

6. Click the Help and Support home button that displays on the Command bar. (This displays the opening Windows Help and Support window.)

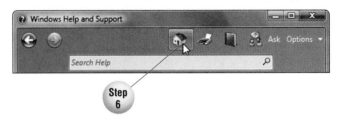

Step 6

7. Click the *What's new* option in the *Find an answer* section.
8. Read the information about Windows Vista that displays in the window.
9. Print the information by clicking the Print button on the Command bar.
10. At the Print dialog box, click the Print button.
11. Click the Help and Support home button on the Command bar.
12. Click the *Table of Contents* option in the *Find an answer* section of the Help window.

Step 9

13. At the list of Windows Vista contents, click the *Files and folders* option.
14. Click the *Working with files and folders* option.
15. Read the information that displays in the Help window on working with files and folders.
16. Click the Help and Support home button on the Command bar.
17. Use the *Search Help* text box to search for information on deleting files by completing the following steps:
    a. Click in the *Search Help* text box.
    b. Type deleting files and then press Enter.
    c. Click the *Delete a file or folder* option that displays in the Help window.

Step 17b

Step 17c

    d. Read the information about deleting files that displays in the Help window.
18. Click the Help and Support home button on the Command bar.
19. Click the Close button located in the upper right corner of the window to close the Windows Help and Support window.

Customizing Settings

Before beginning computer projects in this textbook, you may need to customize the monitor settings and turn on the display of file extensions. Projects in the chapters in this textbook assume that the monitor display is set to 1024 by 768 pixels and that the display of file extensions is turned on. To change the monitor display to 1024 by 768, complete the following steps:

1. At the Windows Vista desktop, right-click on any empty location on the desktop and then click *Personalize* at the shortcut menu.
2. At the Personalization window, click the *Display Settings* option.
3. At the Display Settings dialog box, make sure the screen resolution is set at *1024 by 768 pixels.* If it is not, drag the slider bar button in the *Resolution* section to the left or right until *1024 by 768 pixels* displays below the slider bar.
4. Click the Apply button.
5. Click the Yes button.
6. Click the OK button.
7. Close the Personalization window.

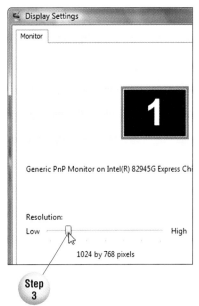

Step 3

To turn on the display of file extensions, complete the following steps:

1. At the Windows Vista desktop, click the Start button and then click *Computer*.
2. At the Computer window, click the Organize button on the Command bar and then click *Folder and Search Options* at the drop-down list.

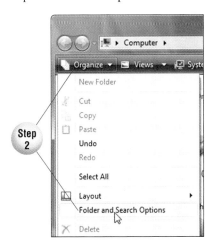

Step 2

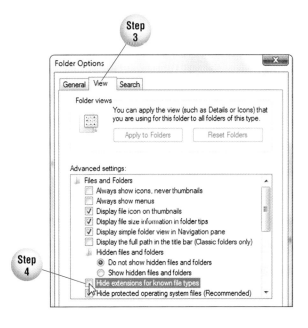

Step 3

Step 4

3. At the Folder Options dialog box, click the View tab.
4. Click the *Hide extensions for known file types* check box to remove the check mark.
5. Click the Apply button.
6. Click the OK button.
7. Close the Computer window.

Browsing the Internet
Using Internet Explorer 7.0

Microsoft Internet Explorer 7.0 is a Web browser program with options and features for displaying sites as well as navigating and searching for information on the Internet. The *Internet* is a network of computers connected around the world. Users access the Internet for several purposes: to communicate using instant messaging and/or e-mail, to subscribe to newsgroups, to transfer files, to socialize with other users around the globe in "chat" rooms, and also to access virtually any kind of information imaginable.

Tutorial IE1
Browsing the Internet with Internet Explorer 7.0
Tutorial IE2
Gathering and Downloading Information and Files

Using the Internet, people can find a phenomenal amount of information for private or public use. To use the Internet, three things are generally required: an Internet Service Provider (ISP), a program to browse the Web (called a *Web browser*), and a *search engine*. In this section, you will learn how to:

- Navigate the Internet using URLs and hyperlinks
- Use search engines to locate information
- Download Web pages and images

Browsing the Internet

You will use the Microsoft Internet Explorer Web browser to locate information on the Internet. Uniform Resource Locators, referred to as URLs, are the method used to identify locations on the Internet. The steps for browsing the Internet vary but generally include: opening Internet Explorer, typing the URL for the desired site, navigating the various pages of the site, navigating to other sites using links, and then closing Internet Explorer.

To launch Internet Explorer 7.0, double-click the *Internet Explorer* icon on the Windows desktop. Figure IE.1 identifies the elements of the Internet Explorer, version 7.0, window. The Web page that displays in your Internet Explorer window may vary from what you see in Figure IE.1.

Figure IE.1 Internet Explorer Window

Title bar

Navigation bar

Address bar

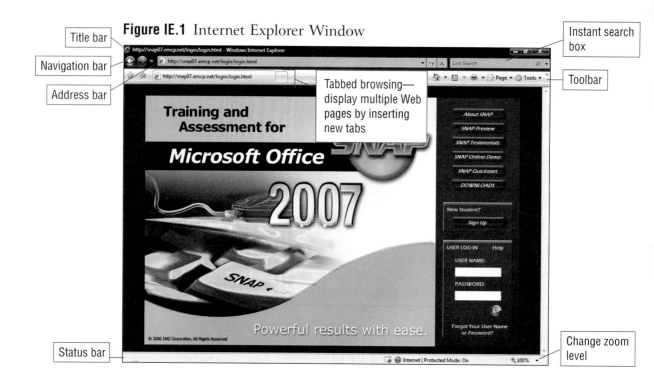

Instant search box

Toolbar

Tabbed browsing—display multiple Web pages by inserting new tabs

Status bar

Change zoom level

If you know the URL for the desired Web site, click in the Address bar, type the URL, and then press Enter. The Web site's home page displays in a tab within the Internet Explorer window. URLs (Uniform Resource Locators) are the method used to identify locations on the Internet. The format of a URL is *http://server-name.path*. The first part of the URL, *http*, stands for HyperText Transfer Protocol, which is the protocol or language used to transfer data within the World Wide Web. The colon and slashes separate the protocol from the server name. The server name is the second component of the URL. For example, in the URL http://www.microsoft.com, the server name is *microsoft*. The last part of the URL specifies the domain to which the server belongs. For example, *.com* refers to "commercial" and establishes that the URL is a commercial company. Other examples of domains include *.edu* for "educational," *.gov* for "government," and *.mil* for "military."

Project ① Browsing the Internet Using URLs

1. Make sure you are connected to the Internet through an Internet Service Provider and that the Windows desktop displays. (Check with your instructor to determine if you need to complete steps for accessing the Internet such as typing a user name and password to log on.)
2. Launch Microsoft Internet Explorer by double-clicking the *Internet Explorer* icon located on the Windows desktop.
3. At the Internet Explorer window, explore the Web site for Yosemite National Park by completing the following steps:
   a. Click in the Address bar, type **www.nps.gov/yose**, and then press Enter.

Step 3a

b. Scroll down the home page for Yosemite National Park by clicking the down-pointing arrow on the vertical scroll bar located at the right side of the Internet Explorer window.

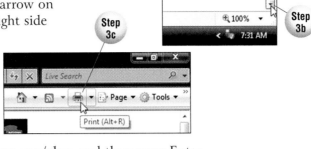

Step 3c

Step 3b

c. Print the home page by clicking the Print button located on the Internet Explorer toolbar.

4. Explore the Web site for Glacier National Park by completing the following steps:

a. Click in the Address bar, type **www.nps.gov/glac**, and then press Enter.

Step 4a

b. Print the home page by clicking the Print button located on the Internet Explorer toolbar.

5. Close Internet Explorer by clicking the Close button (contains an X) located in the upper right corner of the Internet Explorer window.

Navigating Using Hyperlinks

Most Web pages contain "hyperlinks" that you click to connect to another page within the Web site or to another site on the Internet. Hyperlinks may display in a Web page as underlined text in a specific color or as images or icons. To use a hyperlink, position the mouse pointer on the desired hyperlink until the mouse pointer turns into a hand, and then click the left mouse button. Use hyperlinks to navigate within and between sites on the Internet. The navigation bar in the Internet Explorer window contains a Back button that, when clicked, takes you to the previous Web page viewed. If you click the Back button and then want to return to the previous page, click the Forward button. You can continue clicking the Back button to back your way out of several linked pages in reverse order since Internet Explorer maintains a history of the Web sites you visit.

Project ② Navigating Using Hyperlinks

1. Make sure you are connected to the Internet and then double-click the *Internet Explorer* icon on the Windows desktop.

2. At the Internet Explorer window, display the White House Web page and navigate in the page by completing the following steps:

a. Click in the Address bar, type **whitehouse.gov**, and then press Enter.

b. At the White House home page, position the mouse pointer on a hyperlink that interests you until the pointer turns into a hand, and then click the left mouse button.

c. At the linked Web page, click the Back button. (This returns you to the White House home page.)

Step 2c

d. At the White House home page, click the Forward button to return to the previous Web page viewed.

e. Print the Web page by clicking the Print button on the Internet Explorer toolbar.

3. Display the Web site for Amazon.com and navigate in the site by completing the following steps:

a. Click in the Address bar, type www.amazon.com, and then press Enter.

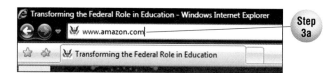

b. At the Amazon.com home page, click a hyperlink related to books.

c. When a book Web page displays, click the Print button on the Internet Explorer toolbar.

4. Close Internet Explorer by clicking the Close button (contains an X) located in the upper right corner of the Internet Explorer window.

Searching for Specific Sites

If you do not know the URL for a specific site or you want to find information on the Internet but do not know what site to visit, complete a search with a search engine. A search engine is a software program created to search quickly and easily for desired information. A variety of search engines are available on the Internet, each offering the opportunity to search for specific information. One method for searching for information is to click in the *Instant Search* box (displays the text *Live Search*) located at the right end of the navigation bar, type a keyword or phrase related to your search, and then click the Search button or press Enter. Another method for completing a search is to visit the Web site for a search engine and use options at the site.

Project ③ Searching for Information by Topic

1. Start Internet Explorer.

2. At the Internet Explorer window, search for sites on bluegrass music by completing the following steps:

a. Click in the *Instant Search* box (may display with *Live Search*) located at the right side of the of the navigation bar.

b. Type **bluegrass music** and then press Enter.

c. When a list of sites displays in the Live Search tab, click a site that interests you.

d. When the page displays, click the Print button.

3. Use the Yahoo! search engine to find sites on bluegrass music by completing the following steps:
   a. Click in the Address bar, type www.yahoo.com, and then press Enter.
   b. At the Yahoo! Web site, with the insertion point positioned in the *Search* text box, type **bluegrass music** and then press Enter. (Notice that the sites displayed vary from sites displayed in the earlier search.)

   c. Click hyperlinks until a Web site displays that interests you.   **Step 3b**
   d. Print the page.
4. Use the Google search engine to find sites on jazz music by completing the following steps:
   a. Click in the Address bar, type www.google.com, and then press Enter.
   b. At the Google Web site, with the insertion point positioned in the search text box, type **jazz music** and then press Enter.

   c. Click a site that interests you.   **Step 4b**
   d. Print the page.
5. Close Internet Explorer.

Completing Advanced Searches for Specific Sites

The Internet contains an enormous amount of information. Depending on what you are searching for on the Internet and the search engine you use, some searches can result in several thousand "hits" (sites). Wading through a large number of sites can be very time-consuming and counterproductive. Narrowing a search to very specific criteria can greatly reduce the number of hits for a search. To narrow a search, use the advanced search options offered by the search engine.

| Web Search |

Project ④ Narrowing a Search

1. Start Internet Explorer.
2. Search for sites on skydiving in Oregon by completing the following steps:
   a. Click in the Address bar and then type www.yahoo.com.
   b. At the Yahoo! Web site, click the Web Search button next to the Search text box and then click the Advanced Search hyperlink.

3. c. At the Advanced Web Search page, click in the search text box next to *all of these words*.
   d. Type skydiving Oregon tandem static line. (This limits the search to Web pages containing all of the words typed in the search text box.)

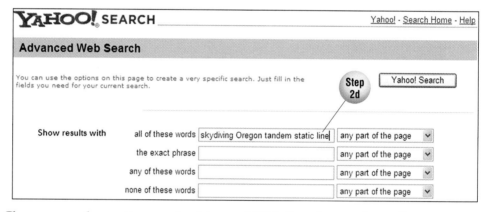

   e. Choose any other options at the Advanced Web Search page that will narrow your search.
   f. Click the Yahoo! Search button.
   g. When the list of Web sites displays, click a hyperlink that interests you.
   h. Print the page.
3. Close Internet Explorer.

Downloading Images, Text, and Web Pages from the Internet

The image(s) and/or text that display when you open a Web page as well as the Web page itself can be saved as a separate file. This separate file can be viewed, printed, or inserted in another file. The information you want to save in a separate file is downloaded from the Internet by Internet Explorer and saved in a folder of your choosing with the name you specify. Copyright laws protect much of the information on the Internet. Before using information downloaded from the Internet, check the site for restrictions. If you do use information, make sure you properly cite the source.

Project ⑤   Downloading Images and Web Pages

1. Start Internet Explorer.
2. Download a Web page and image from Banff National Park by completing the following steps:
   a. Search for sites on the Internet for Banff National Park.
   b. From the list of sites that displays, choose a site that contains information about Banff National Park and at least one image of the park.
   c. Save the Web page as a separate file by clicking the Page button on the Internet Explorer toolbar, and then clicking *Save As* at the drop-down list.
   d. At the Save Webpage dialog box, type **BanffWebPage**.
   e. Navigate to the drive containing your storage medium and then click the Save button. (If the Content pane is not visible, click the Browse Folders button located in the lower left side of the dialog box.)

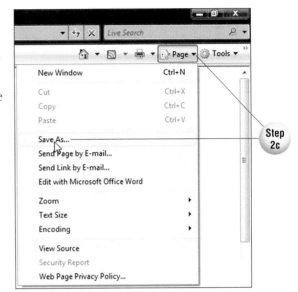

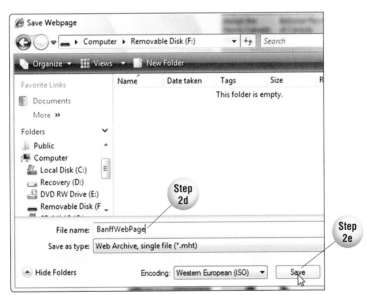

3. Save an image file by completing the following steps:
   a. Right-click an image that displays on the Web site. (The image that displays may vary from what you see at the right.)
   b. At the shortcut menu that displays, click *Save Picture As*.

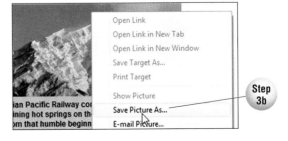

c. At the Save Picture dialog box, type BanffImage.

d. Navigate to the drive containing your storage medium and then click the Save button. (If the Content pane is not visible, click the Browse Folders button.)

4. Close Internet Explorer.

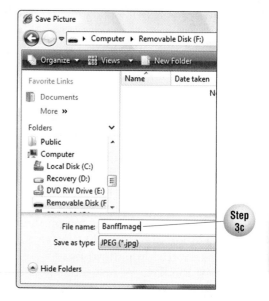

Step 3c

OPTIONAL

Project   Opening the Saved Web Page and Image in a Word Document

1. Open Microsoft Word by clicking the Start button on the Taskbar, pointing to *All Programs*, clicking *Microsoft Office*, and then clicking *Microsoft Office Word 2007*.

2. With Microsoft Word open, insert the image in a document by completing the following steps:

a. Click the Insert tab and then click the Picture button in the Illustrations group.

b. At the Insert Picture dialog box, navigate to the drive containing your storage medium and then double-click *BanffImage.jpg*.

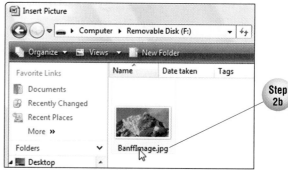

Step 2b

c. When the image displays in the Word document, print the document by clicking the Print button on the Quick Access toolbar.

d. Close the document by clicking the Office button and then clicking *Close* at the drop-down list. At the message asking if you want to save the changes, click No.

3. Open the **BanffWebPage.mht** file by completing the following steps:

a. Click the Office button and then click *Open* at the drop-down menu.

b. At the Open dialog box, navigate to the drive containing your storage medium and then double-click *BanffWebPage.mht*.

Step 3b

c. Print the Web page by clicking the Print button on the Quick Access toolbar.

d. Close the **BanffWebPage.mht** file by clicking the Office button and then *Close*.

4. Close Word by clicking the Close button (contains an X) that displays in the upper right corner of the screen.

Office 2007 – Integrated Project

Now that you have completed the chapters in this textbook, you have learned to create documents in Word, build worksheets in Excel, organize data in Access, and design presentations in PowerPoint. To learn the various programs in the Microsoft Office 2007 suite, you have completed a variety of projects, assessments, and activities. This integrated project is a final assignment that allows you to apply the knowledge you have gained about the programs in the Office suite to produce a variety of documents and files.

Situation

You are the vice president of Classique Coffees, a gourmet coffee company. Your company operates two retail stores that sell gourmet coffee and related products to the public. One retail store is located in Seattle, Washington, the other in Tacoma. The company is three years old and has seen approximately a 10- to 20-percent growth in profit each year. Your duties as the vice president of the company include researching the coffee market; studying coffee buying trends; designing and implementing new projects; and supervising the marketing, sales, and personnel managers.

Activity 1 Write Persuasively

Using Word, compose a memo to the president of Classique Coffees, Leslie Steiner, detailing your research and recommendations:

- Research has shown a 20-percent growth in the iced coffee market.
- The target population for iced coffees is people from ages 18 to 35.
- Market analysis indicates that only three local retail companies sell iced coffees in the greater Seattle-Tacoma area.
- The recommendation is that Classique Coffees develops a suite of iced coffees for market consumption by early next year. (Be as persuasive as possible.)

Save the completed memo and name it **ProjectAct01**. Print and then close **ProjectAct01.docx**.

Activity 2 Design a Letterhead

You are not satisfied with the current letterhead used by your company. Design a new letterhead for Classique Coffees using Word and include the following information:

- Use a clip art image in the letterhead. (Consider downloading a clip art image from Microsoft Office Online.)
- Include the company name—Classique Coffees.
- Include the company address—355 Pioneer Square, Seattle, WA 98211.
- Include the company telephone number—(206) 555-6690.
- Include the company e-mail address—ccoffees@emcp.net.
- Create a slogan that will help your business contacts remember your company.
- Add any other information or elements that you feel are appropriate.

When the letterhead is completed, save it and name it **ProjectAct02**. Print and then close **ProjectAct02.docx**.

Activity 3 **Prepare a Notice**

Using Word, prepare a notice about an upcoming marketing seminar. Include the following information in the notice:

- Name of the seminar—Marketing to the Coffee Gourmet
- Location of the seminar—Conference room at the corporate office, 355 Pioneer Square, Seattle, WA 98211
- Date and time of seminar—Friday, October 19, 2010, 9:00 a.m. to 2:30 p.m.
- Topics that will be covered at the seminar:
    > identifying coffee-drinking trends
    > assessing the current gourmet coffee market
    > developing new products
    > analyzing the typical Classique Coffees customer
    > marketing a new product line
- Consider including a clip art image in the notice. (You determine an appropriate clip art image.)

When the notice is completed, save it and name it **ProjectAct03**. Print and then close **ProjectAct03.docx**.

Activity 4 **Create an Organizational Chart**

In preparation for an upcoming meeting, you need to prepare an organizational chart for the organization of the leadership team at Classique Coffees. Create an organizational chart using a SmartArt graphic that includes the following:

President

Vice President

Marketing Manager   Sales Manager   Personnel Manager

Marketing Assistants   Sales Associates   Assistant Manager

Apply formatting to improve the visual appeal of the chart. Save the chart and name it **ProjectAct04**. Print and then close **ProjectAct04.docx**.

Activity 5 Create a SmartArt Graphic

In addition to the organizational chart, you also want to create a SmartArt graphic that illustrates the steps in a marketing plan. Those steps are:

- Planning
- Development
- Marketing
- Distribution

Apply formatting to improve the visual appeal of the graphic. Save the SmartArt graphic and name it **ProjectAct05**. Print and then close **ProjectAct05.docx**.

Activity 6 Build a Budget Worksheet

Using Excel, prepare a worksheet with the following information:

Annual Budget: $1,450,000

Department	Percent of Budget	Total
Administration	10%	
Purchasing	24%	
Sales	21%	
Marketing	23%	
Personnel	12%	
Training	10%	

Insert formulas that will calculate the total amount for each department based on the specified percentage of the annual budget. When the worksheet is completed, save it and name it **ProjectAct06** and then print **ProjectAct06.xlsx**.

Determine the impact of a 10-percent increase in the annual budget on the total amount for each department. With the amounts displayed for a 10-percent increase, save, print, and then close **ProjectAct06.xlsx**.

Activity 7 Determine Sales Quota Increases

The Marketing Department for Classique Coffees employs seven employees who market the company products to customers. These employees are given a quota for yearly sales that they are to meet. You have determined that the quota needs to be raised for the upcoming year. You are not sure whether the quotas should be increased 5 percent or 10 percent. Using Excel, prepare a worksheet with the following information:

CLASSIQUE COFFEES
Sales Quotas

Employee	Current Quota	Projected Quota
Berenstein	$125,000	
Evans	$100,000	
Grayson	$110,000	

Lueke	$135,000
Nasson	$125,000
Phillips	$150,000
Samuels	$175,000

Insert a formula to determine the projected quotas at 5 percent more than the current quota. Save the worksheet and name it **ProjectAct07A** and then print **ProjectAct07A.xlsx**. Determine the projected quotas at 10 percent more than the current quota. Save the worksheet and name it **ProjectAct07B**. Print and then close **ProjectAct07B.xlsx**.

Activity 8 Build a Sales Worksheet and Create a Chart

Using Excel, prepare a worksheet with the following information:

Type of Coffee	Percent of Sales
Regular blend	22%
Espresso blend	12%
Regular blend decaf	17%
Espresso blend decaf	10%
Flavored blend	25%
Flavored blend decaf	14%

Save the completed worksheet and name it **ProjectAct08** and then print **ProjectAct08.docx**. With the worksheet still displayed, create a pie chart as a new sheet with the data in the worksheet. Title the pie chart *Year 2010 Percentage of Sales*. When the chart is completed, save the worksheet (now two sheets) with the same name (**ProjectAct08.docx**). Print only the sheet containing the pie chart and then close **ProjectAct08.docx**.

Activity 9 Build a Projected Sales Worksheet and Create a Chart

Using Excel, prepare a worksheet with the following information:

Type of Coffee	Percent of Sales
Regular blend	21%
Espresso blend	10%
Regular blend decaf	16%
Espresso blend decaf	8%
Flavored blend	24%
Flavored blend decaf	13%
Iced	5%
Iced decaf	3%

Create a pie chart as a new sheet with the data in the worksheet. Title the pie chart *Year 2011 Projected Percentage of Sales*. When the chart is completed, save the worksheet (two sheets) and name it **ProjectAct09**. Print and then close **ProjectAct09.xlsx**.

Analyze the sales data by comparing and contrasting the pie charts created in **ProjectAct08.xlsx** and **ProjectAct09.xlsx**. What areas in the projected sales percentages have changed? What do these changes indicate? Assume that the projected 2011 annual income for Classique Coffees is $2,200,000. What amount of that income will come from iced coffees (including decaf iced coffees)? Does this amount warrant marketing this new product? Prepare a memo in Word to Leslie Steiner that includes your analysis. Add any other interpretations you can make from analyzing the pie charts. Save the memo and name it **WordProject09**. Print and then close **WordProject09.docx**.

Activity 10 Design and Create a Presentation

Using PowerPoint, prepare a marketing slide presentation. Include the following information in the presentation:

- Classique Coffees 2011 Marketing Plan (title)
- Company reorganization (insert the organizational chart you created in Activity 4)
- 2010 sales percentages (insert into the slide the pie chart that is part of the **ProjectAct08.xlsx** worksheet)
- 2011 projected sales percentages (insert into the slide the pie chart that is part of the **ProjectAct09.xlsx** worksheet)
- Iced coffee marketing strategy
    > target customer
    > analysis of competition
    > wholesale resources
    > pricing
    > volume
- Product placement
    > stocking strategies
    > shelf allocation
    > stock rotation schedule
    > seasonal display

When preparing the slide presentation, you determine the presentation design theme and the layouts. Include any clip art images that might be appropriate and apply an animation scheme to all slides. When the presentation is completed, save it and name it **ProjectAct10**. Run the presentation and then print the presentation with six slides on a page.

Activity 11 Create a Database File and Organize Data

Use Access to create a database for Classique Coffees that contains information on suppliers and products. Include the following fields in the Suppliers table and the Products table (you determine the specific field names):

Suppliers table:
> *Supplier#*
> *SupplierName*
> *Address*
> *City*

State
ZipCode
Email

Products table:
 Product#
 Product
 Supplier#

Type the following data in the Suppliers table:

Supplier#	=	24		*Supplier#*	=	62
SupplierName	=	Gourmet Blends		*SupplierName*	=	Sure Shot Supplies
Address	=	109 South Madison		*Address*	=	291 Pacific Avenue
City	=	Seattle		*City*	=	Tacoma
State	=	WA		*State*	=	WA
ZipCode	=	98032		*ZipCode*	=	98418
Email	=	gblends@emcp.net		*Email*	=	sssupplies@emcp.net
Supplier#	=	36		*Supplier#*	=	41
SupplierName	=	Jannsen Company		*SupplierName*	=	Bertolinos
Address	=	4122 South Sprague		*Address*	=	11711 Meridian East
City	=	Tacoma		*City*	=	Seattle
State	=	WA		*State*	=	WA
ZipCode	=	98402		*ZipCode*	=	98109
Email	=	jannsen@emcp.net		*Email*	=	bertolino@emcp.net

Type the following data in the Products table:

Product#	=	12A-0		*Product#*	=	59R-1
Product	=	Premium blend		*Product*	=	Vanilla syrup
Supplier#	=	24		*Supplier#*	=	62
Product#	=	12A-1		*Product#*	=	59R-2
Product	=	Cappuccino blend		*Product*	=	Raspberry syrup
Supplier#	=	24		*Supplier#*	=	62
Product#	=	12A-2		*Product#*	=	59R-3
Product	–	Hazelnut blend		*Product*	=	Chocolate syrup
Supplier#	=	24		*Supplier#*	=	62
Product#	=	21B-2		*Product#*	=	89T-3
Product	=	12-oz cup		*Product*	=	Napkins, 500 ct
Supplier#	=	36		*Supplier#*	=	41

Product#	=	21B-3	Product#	=	89T-4
Product	=	16-oz cup	Product	=	6-inch stir stick
Supplier#	=	36	Supplier#	=	41

Print both the Suppliers table and the Products table in landscape orientation. Prepare a report with the following information: supplier name, supplier #, supplier e-mail, and product.

Merge the records of those suppliers that are located in Tacoma to a blank Word document. You determine the fields to use in the inside address and an appropriate salutation. Compose a business letter that you will send to the contacts in Tacoma that includes the following information:

- Explain that Classique Coffees is interested in selling iced coffees in the greater Seattle/Tacoma area.
- Ask if the company offers any iced coffee products.
- If the company does not currently offer any iced coffee products, will these products be available in the future?
- Ask the company to send any materials on current products and specifically on iced coffees.
- Ask someone at the company to contact you at the Classique Coffees address, by telephone at (206) 555-6690, or by e-mail at ccoffees@emcp.net.
- Include any other information you think appropriate to the topic.

Merge to a new document and then save the document with the name **ProjectAct11**. Print and then close **ProjectAct11.docx**. Save the main document as **IcedCoffeeLtrMD** and then close **IcedCoffeeLtrMD.docx**.

Activity 12 Assess Your Work

Review the documents you developed and assess your own work in writing. In order to develop an objective perspective of your work, openly solicit constructive criticism from your teacher, peers, and contacts outside of school. Your self-assessment document should specify the weaknesses and strengths of each piece and your specific recommendations for revision and improvement.